Alone With God
In 22 Steps

Proverbs 31

First Edition

Copyright © 19 October 2018 Marah Saruchera

All rights reserved. No part of this publication may be reproduced, stored in any retrieval, or transmitted in any form or by any means, electronic, mechanical photocopying, recording or otherwise, without the prior written consent of the author and production team. Reference to or use of the contents is permitted in instances of non-commercial use permitted by copyright law and/or brief quotations.

Where biblical text is referenced, any one of the following bible versions can be used:
King James Version
New King James Version
New International Version
Revised Standard Version

ISBN 978-0-7974-9722-1

Cover Art and Book Design by:
Enhance Graphics
enhancegraphix@gmail.com

CONTENTS

Preface		4
Introduction		5
Step 1	No Price Tag	10
Step 2	Treasure in Earthen Vessel	19
Step 3	Unwavering Commitment	34
Step 4	Excellent Attitude	46
Step 5	Open Minded	65
Step 6	Proactive Far Sightedness	90
Step 7	Huge Self Esteem	100
Step 8	Positive	117
Step 9	Rejects Mediocrity	128
Step 10	In Control	141
Step 11	Saintly	160
Step 12	Abundant Faith	170
Step 13	Elegant Independence	180
Step 14	Quiet Influence	184

She Is Clothed With Strength And Dignity And Laughs Without Fear Of The Future

Step 15	Enterprising	195
Step 16	Moral Intelligence	203
Step 17	Emotional Intelligence	213
Step 18	Strong Work Ethic	223
Step 19	Grateful	234
Step 20	Unparalleled Integrity	242
Step 21	Self-Sacrificing Humility	252
Step 22	Powerful Sense of Self	260
Conclusion	Queen Of The South	268
References		278

She Is Clothed With Strength And Dignity And Laughs Without Fear Of The Future

PREFACE

The women, who are the subject of this book, do not seek or follow advice, or counsel, that come from sources that do not know or acknowledge God; they neither expect nor support the collusions of the imprudent; they are not comfortable in the midst of, nor do they entertain, the contemptuous.

These women are clothed with strength and dignity, and laugh without fear of the future.

Their conversations, their steps, are ordered by the Lord.

Proverbs 14:15 *The simple believe anything, but the prudent give thought to their steps.*

INTRODUCTION

Prudent, is a woman that knows God.

Solomon was a wise man, but he acknowledges that wiser is a woman that fears God.

A definition of prudent is simple – judicious, practical, sensible, wise, careful, cautious, discreet.

Well known women of the Bible like Esther, Ruth, Abigail, Mary the mother of Jesus, Dorcas, wore prudence just as today's women wear shoes – no one leaves the house barefooted.

Prudent women have a firm foundation – they spend time alone with God. The Lord is their source of confidence. They do not boast; they acknowledge God's provision and enduring mercies.

These women find strength in prayer, they are not ordinary, they are bold, and they are graceful and grateful.

Their intention, their mind-set, is clear. They have self-discipline and self-restraint. They have emotional and moral intelligence, they move away from compromising positions.

Prudent women are in control, not proud, not condescending, but exceptional treasures in earthen vessels.

She Is Clothed With Strength And Dignity And Laughs Without Fear Of The Future

These women reject doubt, fear and resentment – they have a positively powerful sense of self.

These women self-introspect. They know who they are, know where they are coming from, know where they are going.

These women know they cannot reject God, as **Hosea 4:6** says

My people are destroyed for lack of knowledge: because thou hast rejected knowledge, I will also reject thee, that thou shalt be no priest to me: seeing thou hast forgotten the law of thy God, I will also forget thy children. And

These women know their strengths, they know their weaknesses. They acknowledge that the fear of God is the beginning of wisdom.

They are not afraid, they praise, they sing, because they know what it means when they say;

> When you're up against a wall
> And your mountain seems so tall
> And you realize that life's not always fair
> You can run away and hide
> Let the old man decide
> Or you can change your circumstances with a prayer
> When everything falls apart
> Praise his name
>
> When you have a broken heart
> Raise your hands and say
> Lord, you're all I need

You're everything to me
And he'll take the pain away
When it seems you're all alone
Praise his name

And when you feel you can't go on
Raise your hands and say
Greater is he that is within me
And you can praise the hurt away
If you'll just praise his name

Ohhh,
You can overcome
By the blood of the lamb
And by the word of your testimony
You'll see the darkness go
As your faith begins to grow
You're not alone, so how can you be lonely
When everything falls apart
Praise his name

When you have a broken heart
Raise your hands and say
Lord, you're all I need
You're everything to me
And he'll take the pain away
When it seems you're all alone
Praise his name

And when you feel you can't go on
Raise your hands and say
Greater is he that is within me
And you can praise the hurt away
Greater is he that is within me
And you can praise the hurt away
If you'll just praise his name

Jeff and Sheri Easter and Charlotte Ritchie

She Is Clothed With Strength And Dignity And Laughs Without Fear Of The Future

These women's mantra, their payoff line is; not by power, nor by might, but by the Spirit of the Lord.

Together with these women, we say; we are what we are because Christ died for us, we do what we do because Christ did all for us.

We know that neither salvation nor wealth are from our works, they are gifts from God through Christ Jesus.

Even though our works are as filthy rags, and our works do not save us; we still put our hands to the plough, because we refuse the bread of idleness.

This book highlights the fact that a woman who spends time with God does not need a crowd to authenticate her.

She is the person David says in **Psalms 1:1-3**

¹Blessed is the man (generic) that walketh not in the counsel of the unGodly, nor standeth in the way of sinners, nor sitteth in the seat of the scornful.² But his delight is in the law of the LORD; and in his law doth he meditate day and night.³ And he shall be like a tree planted by the rivers of water, that bringeth forth his fruit in his season; his leaf also shall not wither; and whatsoever he doeth shall prosper.

She Is Clothed With Strength And Dignity And Laughs Without Fear Of The Future

Her steps cannot be mistaken, for she walks with her God, the Creator of the Universe, the Giver of Life.

This is an "all together woman". She is intentional.

A woman who spends time with God can be understood, for her intentions are pure.

This is the woman who is the subject of this book.

STEP 1

NO PRICE TAG

Proverbs 31:10 asks *Who can find a virtuous woman? for her price is far above rubies.*

Price is a tag for exchange. One who has an item, big or small, put a price tag on it. The tag may be made public or displayed, or it can be a matter of the heart.

Where the price is displayed for public interest, this is normally done for a few reasons:

Exchange value – one wants to put a price so they can get something of equivalent value.

Disposal – one just wants to get rid of the item. The item may no longer be of value to the owner, so the owner decides, someone may still use it, but I can't give it out for free.

Net worth – someone wants to know how valuable the item is. In such instances, the owner will pay out a significant sum of money to get someone else – an expert in dealing with that product or item – to place a value on the owner's particular finished or unique item.

Growth – one is interested in knowing how their item increased in value over time.

Assess performance – how is the item performing in comparison to other similar and comparable items.

Definitions derived from Google Free Dictionary

When Solomon sat to think and reflect on women, he came up with a short question – who can find a virtuous woman – for her price is far above rubies.

It took him time and he was at pains to explain that a good, righteous, worthy, honourable, moral, upright and honest woman is really hard to find.

In other words, out of his seven hundred woman and three hundred concubines, Solomon had failed to find a virtuous woman – or was there one?

We know Solomon's wives were many, but there is one the Bible mentions in more detail – Pharaoh's daughter.

The daughter of the Egyptian Pharaoh **[1 Kings 9:16; 2 Chronicles 8:11]** Solomon took for a wife because he wanted to cement a political alliance.

Really?

One can ask, where had Solomon left his God, to think he needed a Pharaoh to defeat his enemies – inside or outside of his kingdom.

1 Kings 3:1, as quoted from *Women In the Scriptures*, it took twenty years for Solomon to finish building the palace he would give to Pharaoh's daughter for a house. This woman had no name (probably Nicaule or Tashere according to Bible scholars), she is simply called Pharaoh's daughter. Her father burnt Gezer (a city) with fire so he could give his daughter the city for a present!

From **1 Kings 11**, Solomon's wives came from Moab, the Ammonite women – such as Naamah the mother of Rehoboam **[2 Chronicles 12:13]**, and from Edom, Zidon and other Canaanite nations.

Is it possible then, that Solomon married so many women because he failed to find one who was virtuous?

This is very plausible, because all the women he married were foreign, no one knew the God of Israel - our God – so no one could be virtuous, that is why they got to be a thousand women "married" to one man!

A virtuous woman cannot be exchanged or disposed of; her net worth is beyond her, her growth unsearchable and her performance incomparable.

First Kings 11 says

In God Alone

"But king Solomon loved many strange women, together with the daughter of Pharaoh, women of the Moabites, Ammonites, Edomites, Zidonians, and Hittites:

Strange is a very hard word, especially coming from the Bible.

A strange woman means a woman the Bible is at pains to describe. She is odd, bizarre, outlandish, eccentric, weird, negatively extraordinary and peculiar in a very odd way. She is abnormal.

When a woman is of this nature, she will be very easy to dispose of. No one is safe with her – she dresses anyhow, speaks anyhow, walks anyhow. She is an anyhow woman.

This is because her gods are the gods of this world. She lives in an "anything goes" world. She acts sick and has a bad attitude.

She is sloppy and unkempt. She is strange because she has no time for God.

A woman who spends time alone with God makes conversation with God, self-introspecting, frequently asking herself – who am I?

A virtuous woman is a Godly woman. She knows she is a child of God first, her father's daughter!

She Is Clothed With Strength And Dignity And Laughs Without Fear Of The Future

²*Of the nations concerning which the* LORD *said unto the children of Israel, Ye shall not go in to them, neither shall they come in unto you: for surely they will turn away your heart after their gods: Solomon clave unto these in love.*

³*And he had seven hundred wives, princesses, and three hundred concubines: and his wives turned away his heart.*

Strange women have capacity to turn hearts after *their gods*. In their anyhow world, they can twist and turn until they get whoever will to their equally strange gods – which gods have eyes but cannot see, who have ears but cannot hear.

A priceless woman will pray – "remove the eye salve in my eyes oh God, that I may see as you want me to". This prayer is not a public prayer. It's an alone with God prayer.

A woman that stays in God's presence knows which company to join. Mixed multitudes are always a "stay away from".

Moabites are in the mixed multitudes – a people born out of drunken stupor. This is the reason they created their own god Chemosh, even though Lot their father had known the God of Israel.

And so were the Ammonites, with their god Milcom.

This is according to Joel S Burnet.

Edomites – descendants of Esau, had their god too Qaus (or Qos)

> Ammon, Moab and Edom: Gods and Kingdoms East of the Jordan
> by *Joel S. Burnett*

Ziddonians were the relatives of Jezebel, the Baal god worshiper. Siddon is what the *Biblical Archaeology Society* has called Jezebel's home town.

From Noah, to Ham to Canaan to Heth, are the Hittites – the offspring of God's people gone bad.

This is a mixed multitude of people that no virtuous woman would want to join.

A woman who stays at the feet of Jesus cannot pretend all is well in this multitude.

There are places where only the daughters of Jezebel can live – daughters of God have an insight into the presence of God.

There is no way Solomon could have found virtue in this congregation.

The Bible further says in **1st Kings 11**

> [4] *For it came to pass, when Solomon was old, that his wives turned away his heart after other gods: and his heart was not perfect with the LORD his God, as was the heart of David his father.*

⁵ For Solomon went after Ashtoreth the goddess of the Zidonians, and after Milcom the abomination of the Ammonites.

⁶ And Solomon did evil in the sight of the LORD, and went not fully after the LORD, as did David his father.

⁷ Then did Solomon build an high place for Chemosh, the abomination of Moab, in the hill that is before Jerusalem, and for Molech, the abomination of the children of Ammon.

⁸ And likewise did he for all his strange wives, which burnt incense and sacrificed unto their gods.

Solomon had the audacity to build a high place (or mini temple) for each of his wives. One can imagine the commotion that prevailed in Solomon's temple complex.

The Bible says Solomon built a palace for Pharaoh's daughter – taking twenty years to build it. Twenty years was half the time Solomon ruled Israel – what a waste!

Women who spend time with God have order. When you lose order, you know the price – a bad ending. Solomon knew better – to whom much is given more is demanded. Solomon had plenty of wisdom – so how could he -

⁹ And the LORD was angry with Solomon, ¹¹ Wherefore the LORD said unto Solomon, Forasmuch as this is done of thee, and thou hast not kept my covenant and my statutes, which I have commanded thee, I will surely rend the kingdom from thee, and will give it to thy servant...... but I will rend it out of the hand of thy son..........13 Howbeit I will not rend away all the kingdom; but will give one tribe to thy son for David my servant's sake, and for Jerusalem's sake which I have chosen....

14 And the LORD stirred up an adversary unto Solomon, Hadad the Edomite: 23 And God stirred him up another adversary, Rezon the son of Eliadah, ...25 And he was an adversary to Israel all the days of Solomon,.26 And Jeroboam the son of Nebat, an Ephrathite of Zereda, Solomon's servant, whose mother's name was Zeruah, a widow woman, even he lifted up his hand against the king.

The Bible text above is an illustration of how bad things got for Solomon.

I will surmise and say, if Solomon had had one priceless woman, who knew God as we ought to, we may be reading a different tale.

Regardless of our earthly father's stature or standing, regardless of our God given talents, God still does respect our choices.

At the end of Solomon's forty years of reigning over Israel, he came to know, that virtue is endowed by God, to men and women who spend time – alone – with God.

In God Alone

If Solomon had found one woman, with no price tag, Solomon's sons would have reigned over Israel and Judah. The woman Solomon could not find, the virtuous woman, only God can create.

In this woman, what you see is what you get. She is not pretentious, she is genuine. She is not Pharaoh's daughter, she is just judicious, practical, sensible, wise, careful, cautious, and discreet.

That woman, is any woman that spends time alone with God.

She does not need validation or applause, she is pretty inside and pretty outside.

She Is Clothed With Strength And Dignity And Laughs Without Fear Of The Future

STEP 2

TREASURE IN EARTHEN VESSEL

Solomon says husbands trust their wives – with their hearts.

However, trust ill placed can spell disaster for families. Trust, as is commonly said, is earned, and it is so easy to lose.

A prudent woman is trusted.

A prudent woman cherishes love – of creatures great and small, of man and man relationships. She does not focus on money and its enablings.

A prudent woman cherishes the love of God and Godly things.

When Solomon wrote **Proverbs 31:11** *The heart of her husband doth safely trust in her, so that he shall have no need of spoil"*, he was probably thinking of Abigail, Nabal's wife.

With Abigail, Nabal needed not look any further, regardless of his own shortcomings, which would have probably have "pushed" him to many women.

Abigal was the epitome of virtue. Abigal was synonymous with benefit, advantage, quality, an asset and an invaluable feature in the family.

The Bible says in

1 Samuel 25:2 *And there was a man in Maon, whose possessions were in Carmel; and the man was very great, and he had three thousand sheep, and a thousand goats: and he was shearing his sheep in Carmel.³ Now the name of the man was Nabal; and the name of his wife Abigail: and she was a woman of good understanding, and of a beautiful countenance: but the man was churlish and evil in his doings; and he was of the house of Caleb."*

The first thing that strikes me from this passage is the mismatch.

How was this ever possible?

From the two verses, we recognise Caleb, a man of God, who had relied and lived and trusted the promises of God to take His people to the Promised Land.

Caleb was a man of repute. In contrast, Nabal was the opposite of Caleb his grandfather.

The Bible gives the genealogy so it is clear how privileged Nabal was, in the physical, yet so destitute in the emotional and spiritual.

In God Alone

Abigail did not consider it significant that Nabal was the man that he was. She considered Nabal was of the house of Caleb, as much as any woman would consider "equal" yoking.

The Bible says Abigail was a woman of good understanding – not just understanding.

This means Abigail was not only sympathetic, empathetic, considerate, thoughtful, kind, accepting, indulgent and appreciative, Abigail was good at all these.

She was built for the purpose, at the right place at the right time – where good understanding was needed in good measure.

In a way, Abigail's work had been cut out for her.

Abigail was treasure in an earthen vessel. Abigail was all of chapter 5, she was a super vessel.

The story goes: -

[4] And David heard in the wilderness that Nabal did shear his sheep.

[5] And David sent out ten young men, and David said unto the young men, Get you up to Carmel, and go to Nabal, and greet him in my name:

She Is Clothed With Strength And Dignity and Laughs Without Fear Of The Future

⁶ And thus shall ye say to him that liveth in prosperity, Peace be both to thee, and peace be to thine house, and peace be unto all that thou hast.

⁷ And now I have heard that thou hast shearers: now thy shepherds which were with us, we hurt them not, neither was there ought missing unto them, all the while they were in Carmel.

⁸ Ask thy young men, and they will shew thee. Wherefore let the young men find favour in thine eyes: for we come in a good day: give, I pray thee, whatsoever cometh to thine hand unto thy servants, and to thy son David.

⁹ And when David's young men came, they spake to Nabal according to all those words in the name of David, and ceased.

¹⁰ And Nabal answered David's servants, and said, Who is David? and who is the son of Jesse? there be many servants now a days that break away every man from his master.

¹¹ Shall I then take my bread, and my water, and my flesh that I have killed for my shearers, and give it unto men, whom I know not whence they be?

¹² So David's young men turned their way, and went again, and came and told him all those sayings.

¹³ And David said unto his men, Gird ye on every man his sword. And they girded on every man his sword; and David also girded on his sword: and there went up after David

about four hundred men; and two hundred abode by the stuff.

¹⁴ *But one of the young men told Abigail, Nabal's wife, saying, Behold, David sent messengers out of the wilderness to salute our master; and he railed on them.*

The same words that were told to Nabal and created a railing or criticizing outcome, were told to Abigail, by a young man in her husband's employ, and created a very different response.

Abigail responded in a way that shows she knew her situation and her husband – and she also knew avoiding a fight is a mark of honour.

Raising the issue with her husband then was going to delay every other decision – and bring on destruction.

She knew when to speak her mind – in season.

¹⁵ *But the men were very good unto us, and we were not hurt, neither missed we anything, as long as we were conversant with them, when we were in the fields:*

¹⁶ *They were a wall unto us both by night and day, all the while we were with them keeping the sheep.*

¹⁷ *Now therefore know and consider what thou wilt do; for evil is determined against our master, and against all his household: for he is such a son of Belial, that a man cannot speak to him.*

Abigail responded appropriately to a threat of evil upon her husband and family.

Abigail had heard about David and his six hundred men. Everyone in Israel knew who David was. She simply responded from the words that her young man had told her. She was a good discerner of the mind.

Wise women read between the lines. They do not take anything for granted. Abigail was a thoughtful woman.

Abigail knew her husband. One cannot understand anything they do not know. When the young man said our master "railed on them", Abigail knew exactly what that meant.

The young man who briefed Abigail knew the woman that Abigail was. He knew he could talk to Abigail and Abigail would listen.

Abigail's handyman knew Abigail would not sit around and moan.

In Abigail's world, there was no time to sigh, even to groan, to whine or to whimper.

Abigail did not discuss her husband with the young man. The young man also knew what Nabal was – a churlish man. Abigail was not there to confirm or refute the young man's belief.

I want to believe, this characterisation of Nabal was known, not only by Abigail and his handyman, his kith and kin knew too, that Nabal was rude and mean spirited.

In that environment, Abigal had no options. She had no choices, she had no alternatives.

Abigail's compass was one directional – God.

In **1 Samuel 25:18** the Bible says

Then Abigail made haste, and took two hundred loaves, and two bottles of wine, and five sheep ready dressed, and five measures of parched corn, and an hundred clusters of raisins, and two hundred cakes of figs, and laid them on asses.

Abigail did not waste time. The stakes were high. Nabal's fall was going to be her fall too. Abigail was to deny David the opportunity to destroy them both.

It's possible the wine was in place, and the parched corn, and the clusters of raisins, but what of two hundred loaves and two hundred cakes of figs. Someone had to do something – fast.

She was a real world, hands on, everyday woman who knew what and how.

[19] *And she said unto her servants, Go on before me; behold, I come after you. But she told not her husband Nabal.*

She Is Clothed With Strength And Dignity and Laughs Without Fear Of The Future

She told not her husband – really? How is that possible? What if, what of....?

Abigail was not rash. She was a woman of good understanding. What was at stake was greater than formalities and wifely courtesy.

Yes, its good manners to tell before you do. By the way, you are someone's wife. You may actually be "Nabal's wife".

Abigail recognized it was "situation critical". It was a life and death situation – you fight for what belongs to you!

The servants knew Abigail was an assured woman.

She was confident. Her actions followed her words. There was no contradiction between her words and her actions.

She says to her servants "go before me, and I will be right behind". The situation did not want a wishy-washy woman.

Abigail was solid. The Almighty God, was Abigail's confidence.

[20] *And it was so, as she rode on the ass, that she came down by the covert on the hill, and, behold, David and his men came down against her; and she met them.*

By the thicket of the hill, *David and his men came down against her.*

Abigail did not run away from David and his four hundred armed men – *she met them.*

The scene must have been breath taking. A woman on an ass meets an army general on the run (an outlaw) and his armed might – discontent man, man in debt, mercenaries, and soldiers of fortune.

Abigail was not intimidated.

21 Now David had said, surely in vain have I kept all that this fellow hath in the wilderness, so that nothing was missed of all that pertained unto him: and he hath requited me evil for good.

22 So and more also do God unto the enemies of David, if I leave of all that pertain to him by the morning light any that pisseth against the wall.

23 And when Abigail saw David, she hasted, and lighted off the ass, and fell before David on her face, and bowed herself to the ground,

Abigail knew how to fight.

She was not going to fight standing.

In that crouched position, Abigail was more powerful than David and four hundred armed outlaws.

She Is Clothed With Strength And Dignity and Laughs Without Fear Of The Future

She was not going to let her face be seen by her enemies. Abigail knew, when you expose yourself, you open yourself up to abuse, to ridicule, to scornful people.

Abigail knew, there is a time to hide your face from enemy attacks.

Abigail knew, when you expose yourself, you should be sure you are on higher ground.

Abigail would plead guilty and save her household.

Her servants must have been smiling behind the curtain of loaded donkeys. They knew – if anyone was going to "rescue" them, it was their Abigail.

24 And fell at his feet, and said, upon me, my Lord, upon me let this iniquity be: and let thine handmaid, I pray thee, speak in thine audience, and hear the words of thine handmaid.

David must have been thinking – how so…?

25 Let not my Lord, I pray thee, regard this man of Belial, even Nabal: for as his name is, so is he; Nabal is his name, and folly is with him: but I thine handmaid saw not the young men of my Lord, whom thou didst send.

…should I have sent them to you…?

Names matter. Nabal had failed, he was just answering to his name.

26 Now therefore, my Lord, as the LORD liveth, and as thy soul liveth, seeing the LORD hath withholden thee from coming to shed blood, and from avenging thyself with thine own hand, now let thine enemies, and they that seek evil to my Lord, be as Nabal.

…really…?

27 And now this blessing which thine handmaid hath brought unto my Lord, let it even be given unto the young men that follow my Lord.

…what blessing…

28 I pray thee, forgive the trespass of thine handmaid: for the LORD will certainly make my Lord a sure house; because my Lord fighteth the battles of the LORD, and evil hath not been found in thee all thy days.

…you sure know me….

29 Yet a man is risen to pursue thee, and to seek thy soul: but the soul of my Lord shall be bound in the bundle of life with the LORD thy God; and the souls of thine enemies, them shall he sling out, as out of the middle of a sling.

…even my battle with Goliath…

30 And it shall come to pass, when the LORD shall have done to my Lord according to all the good that he hath spoken concerning thee, and shall have appointed thee ruler over Israel;

…my anointment too…?

31 That this shall be no grief unto thee, nor offence of heart unto my Lord, either that thou hast shed blood causeless, or that my Lord hath avenged himself: but when the LORD shall have dealt well with my Lord, then remember thine handmaid.

…impressive!

32 And David said to Abigail, blessed be the LORD God of Israel, which sent thee this day to meet me:

33 And blessed be thy advice, and blessed be thou, which hast kept me this day from coming to shed blood, and from avenging myself with mine own hand.

34 For in very deed, as the LORD God of Israel liveth, which hath kept me back from hurting thee, except thou hadst hasted and come to meet me, surely there had not been left unto Nabal by the morning light any that pisseth against the wall.

David says to Abigail – if you had not hasted (quick), your house would be ruins by now.

David was not going to ask. He was going to destroy from the gate that he would have used to come through.

Abigail knew Nabal's household and goods were going to be David's loot before that day had ended.

Abigail's wisdom, knowledge and understanding saved David too – God would not let him.

Abigail bridged the gap between not only Nabal and David, but between David and God too.

I want to believe, Nabal, regardless of his condescending character, knew his wife was priceless.

[35] So David received of her hand that which she had brought him, and said unto her, Go up in peace to thine house; see, I have hearkened to thy voice, and have accepted thy person.

[36] And Abigail came to Nabal; and, behold, he held a feast in his house, like the feast of a king; and Nabal's heart was merry within him, for he was very drunken: wherefore she told him nothing, less or more, until the morning light.

In all situations and circumstances, the morning light will come.

When morning comes, every man will see reason.

A woman of understanding will wait, until the morning light.

Rushing to tell is not wisdom when the man is Nabal – know your person's name.

As long as you know his name, you know how to relate. A name is like a belief system. Know where he comes from.

She Is Clothed With Strength And Dignity and Laughs Without Fear Of The Future

I would say, put on *his* thinking cap.

- When a man is holding a feast in his house – let him alone – he is in his territory.
- When a man has prepared himself the feast of a king – his ego is his kingdom – let him enjoy.
- When a man's heart is merry within him – he can't be bothered by your issues – so don't start.
- When the man is very drunken (by whatever) – wait for the morning light.

37 But it came to pass in the morning, when the wine was gone out of Nabal, and his wife had told him these things, that his heart died within him, and he became as a stone.

38 And it came to pass about ten days after, that the LORD smote Nabal, that he died.

Really - all along the Lord was there!

Yes, God was in it.

39 And when David heard that Nabal was dead, he said, Blessed be the LORD, that hath pleaded the cause of my reproach from the hand of Nabal, and hath kept his servant from evil: for the LORD hath returned the wickedness of Nabal upon his own head. And David sent and communed with Abigail, to take her to him to wife.

Paul was inspired to write in **2 Corinthians 4:7-10,**

7 But we have this treasure in jars of clay to show that this all-surpassing power is from God and not from us. 8We are hard pressed on every side, but not crushed; perplexed, but not in despair; 9 persecuted, but not abandoned; struck down, but not destroyed. 10 We always carry around in our body the death of Jesus, so that the life of Jesus may also be revealed in our body.

The story of Abigail is quite inspiring for women of all ages, regardless of social status, education and spirituality.

I believe, when a woman stands up from the inside, or in the inside, she can challenge any situation and or circumstance.

That stand up confidence, power, wisdom, comes from God.

Women are strong, they are powerful, they are rulers, they are wise, and they are everything the Lord gave.

Godly women are, treasures in earthen vessels.

She Is Clothed With Strength And Dignity and Laughs Without Fear Of The Future

STEP 3

UNWAVERING COMMITMENT

As I looked up this chapter heading, and thinking how the story of Deborah would fit into this chapter, my attention was drawn to the definitions of the words – waver and commit.

From the Oxford Dictionary of Languages, waver is flicker, such as happens when a candle flame is in the wind.

Commitment is dedication to a cause or activity.

It is an engagement or obligation that restricts freedom of action.

Wow.

The combination of these words is significant.

Generally, living needs a level of commitment, to a cause, to an institution, and to beliefs.

However, levels of commitment vary.

Commitment to God, to a husband, to children, to an employer, varies in its type and in its power.

Unwavering commitment means undisturbed focus.

Women, generally, are known to commit to their husbands, even at times, without question.

Culture, belief systems and other societal guidelines, define the level of commitment, to anything and to anyone.

To God – commitment cannot vary and it cannot be slack – God is the Creator of the Universe, the Giver of Life.

The Lord God, is the Author and Finisher of our faith.

Our God, therefore defines our level of commitment to our marriages (marriage as a third party), to our husbands, our children, our work, our everything.

A woman who knows God, as Solomon says in **Proverbs 31:12** *will do him (her husband) good and not evil all the days of her (woman's) life.*

This, to me, is a very powerful statement.

This level of commitment, unfaltering, unwavering, is simply not possible outside God.

God gives this woman power to will and to do.

All days of one's life means exactly that – the commitment and everything that comes with it is huge.

She Is Clothed With Strength And Dignity and Laughs Without Fear Of The Future

Commitment that is bigger and better than what power and influence can bring, even for the likes of Deborah the judge.

Deborah was a judge, probably a judge president. In our day, she would probably be a judge of the Supreme Court.

Regardless, she was someone's wife.

In the book of **Judges 4:4-10** the Bible says

4 And Deborah, a prophetess, the wife of Lapidoth, she judged Israel at that time.

The Bible had to mention Deborah was a wife.

She was a companion, she was a mate, she was a partner to Lapidoth.

By default, Deborah had to be effective and efficient in balancing the demands of being a judge and being a wife.

That is not small calling. It means quick thinking, it means humility, it means wisdom, and it means foresight.

Deborah had to commit, unwavering, to both institutions.

Lapidoth was of Israel. By inference, Deborah "judged" her husband, as Deborah ruled over Israel.

In this Bible context, Lapidoth was a subject to Deborah.

This means there were times when Lapidoth sought counsel from his wife Deborah, not as a wife, but as a subject.

It was Deborah's job to balance the issues – home and office, the two institutions that she was committed to "till death did them part".

Deborah had to commit unwaveringly to her husband, as power would give her the ability to do the opposite of what God called for in her position as a wife.

5 And she dwelt under the palm tree of Deborah between Ramah and Bethel in mount Ephraim: and the children of Israel came up to her for judgment

Deborah had power. Her opinion mattered. Her word was valued.

Deborah gave orders to go to war and in battle she gave the battle cry.

In her court she "gave life".

On her seat she could "take away life".

Deborah worked with God and for God.

She sent for and called army generals, not by their titles but by their names. Deborah had authority.

She Is Clothed With Strength And Dignity and Laughs Without Fear Of The Future

6 And she sent and called Barak the son of Abinoam out of Kedeshnaphtali, and said unto him, Hath not the LORD God of Israel commanded, saying, Go and draw toward mount Tabor, and take with thee ten thousand men of the children of Naphtali and of the children of Zebulun?

7 And I will draw unto thee to the river Kishon Sisera, the captain of Jabin's army, with his chariots and his multitude; and I will deliver him into thine hand.

From verse 6 to 7, by inference, Barak new what he had been told by God, but he had no will power to do so.

Deborah knew exactly what the Lord had said, because she communed with God. She enquired in the Lord's temple.

Deborah asks – has not the Lord commanded you. The wifely nature in her stopped her short of saying "why have you not done what the Lord said you ought to do?"

When men faltered, Deborah stood.

Discerning Barak's fear, Deborah assures Barak, by stating the facts of God's promises.

8 And Barak said unto her, If thou wilt go with me, then I will go: but if thou wilt not go with me, then I will not go.

Deborah led a division, ten thousand men.

She Is Clothed With Strength And Dignity and Laughs Without Fear Of The Future

In God Alone

In today's language, that kind of an army is led by a Major General.

Closer home, Deborah would have likely ranked with the Major Generals of the two world wars.

I do not know if Deborah's army had women, but from Bible records, the women in Israel at that time did not go to war, and the man that did were twenty years and above.

What this says of Deborah is monumental. Deborah was not dealing with or handling small boys.

She was not shying away wondering what other women would think or what her husband would think. She knew she was not any other woman; she was Deborah, a prophetess, a judge and the wife to Lapidoth.

In that position, Deborah had to read the riot act to herself – thou shall do well to your husband all your days. Not the days of her husband, for she had no control over her husband's days – but her days. That meant in good or bad days.

She was fully aware of her responsibilities, to God and to man. Sinking to the lower morality of some women she could not do.

I would not know which division Deborah would "deploy" her husband as they went to war, but

Deborah's husband would be so sure Deborah would be good to him, even on the battlefield.

Deborah's story would be good.

Faced with doubt,

⁹ she said, I will surely go with thee: notwithstanding the journey that thou takest shall not be for thine honour; for the LORD shall sell Sisera into the hand of a woman. And Deborah arose, and went with Barak to Kedesh.

¹⁰ And Barak called Zebulun and Nephtali to Kedesh; and he went up with ten thousand men at his feet: and Deborah went up with him.

Deborah was powerful because she was a prophetess.

Prophets seek God and put God first.

- **Amos 3:7** - *"Surely the Lord GOD will do nothing, but he revealeth his secret unto his servants the prophets."*
- **1 John 4:1** - *"Beloved, believe not every spirit, but try the spirits whether they are of God: because many false prophets are gone out into the world."*
- **2 Peter 1:21** - *"For no prophecy was ever produced by the will of man, but men spoke from God as they were carried along by the Holy Spirit."*

That was Deborah, she was true to her calling, and she was not pretentious.

She Is Clothed With Strength And Dignity and Laughs Without Fear Of The Future

She knew the details of how this war with Sisera, was going to be fought, and how it was going to end.

Deborah did not just commit to her husband, she committed to a nation.

Deborah could stand on top of mount Tabor, because she stood with her God.

The Bible says Deborah judged Israel at the time when the Lord had sold the children of Israel to Jabin king of Canaan, when Sisera was captain.

Deborah fought against the best armies of her time.

The Bible says in **Judges 4:3-4** *And the children of Israel cried unto the LORD: for he had nine hundred chariots of iron; and twenty years he mightily oppressed the children of Israel. And Deborah… she judged Israel at that time.*

That time – was a time when fear reigned in Israel.

How do you fight an enemy with chariots of iron, unless the Lord God fights your battles?

Deborah presided over the war cabinet.

The Book of Judges mentions twelve judges. From Othniel, Ehud, Shamgar, Deborah and Gideon, to Tola, Jair, Jephthah, Ibzan, Elon, Abdan and Samson.

Being a wife and mother is good enough, being a judge of the twelve tribes of Israel is exceptional.

She Is Clothed With Strength And Dignity and Laughs Without Fear Of The Future

In a land where the Lord has given to occupy yet the enemy is everywhere, Deborah had to be strong willed, objective and decisive.

Deborah was in the trenches, behind enemy lines, and alone with God.

As Deborah says in **Judges 5:7**

The inhabitants of the villages ceased, they ceased in Israel, until that I Deborah arose, that I arose a mother in Israel... ¹³the LORD made me have dominion over the mighty.

Deborah's statement is not from pride, it's a testament of fact. Deborah was simply reading aloud her report.

Women of God can sing a song of victory – not in self-praise, but in recognition of a fact – the Lord makes them have dominion over the mighty.

You can only sing that song of triumph, when you do, spend time alone with God.

Judges 3 says

Now these are the nations which the LORD left, to prove Israel by them, even as many of Israel as had not known all the wars of Canaan;

² Only that the generations of the children of Israel might know, to teach them war, at the least such as before knew nothing thereof;

Deborah was raised to bring back to Israel the knowledge of our fighting God.

Deborah was anointed to let the heathens know, that the Lord is God, He goes before us.

This takes a lot of courage and faith – the belief that He who promised is faithful.

It requires men and women who know their God, trusting and listening.

By obedience, these men and women increase their faith.

These men and women pray without ceasing, seeking the face of God.

Life has this "thing" – that there are times, when the Lord leaves foreigners in our midst, to prove us. People who do not speak our faith language, nor pray to our God, people who are not ashamed or constrained in any way, people who prove our being.

3 Namely, five Lords of the Philistines, and all the Canaanites, and the Sidonians, and the Hivites that dwelt in mount Lebanon, from mount Baalhermon unto the entering in of Hamath.

4 And they were to prove Israel by them, to know whether they would hearken unto the commandments of the LORD, which he commanded their fathers by the hand of Moses.

These people want to test the clothes we wear – is it strength, is it dignity?

All the nations that the Lord left to prove Israel were idolatrous, who worshipped all sorts of gods.

The woman who knows God, will know, how to fight such – God left them where they are and God will raise His standard to remove such from their midst, at the appointed time.

Some are left just so we know how to fight, and so we know without God we are helpless.

Without God, our adversaries are mightier than we.

All generations of the children of God ought to know how to fight. Life is not playing marbles.

God knows what He left to prove us. Praying will give us the biggest advantage, and that is all we need, an advantage over our enemies.

God is our hill advantage, for He is the Creator of the Universe, the Giver of Life.

5 And the children of Israel dwelt among the Canaanites, Hittites, and Amorites, and Perizzites, and Hivites, and Jebusites.... 9the LORD raised up a deliverer to the children of Israel, who delivered them, even Othniel the son of Kenaz, Caleb's younger brother

As much as God fulfilled Deborah's days, so will He fulfil the number of our days.

The charge is simple, keep at the ropes; wear strength, wear dignity.

Deborah's commitment to the institutions that looked up to her was remarkable.

It meant she read the riot act to herself, and also wrote her own story – how she won the war against the mighty.

War generals commit, body and soul.

Deborah did, for [13]*the LORD made me have dominion over the mighty.*

This world is a war zone, the war we fight, at home and abroad, is a war of attrition – we are in the trenches for a very long time.

We just need God.

STEP 4

EXCELLENT ATTITUDE

Attitude is an encompassing term that attempts to describe behavioural attributes such as arrogance, boldness, defiance, assertiveness and honourable.

Attitude is a way of thinking or feeling.

Attitude can also be uncooperative behaviour.

A good attitude brings positive outcomes.

An excellent attitude creates behaviour that is exceptional, outstanding and admirable.

Attitude distinguishes people, it separates them.

Employers seek from their employees a work ethic that brings in and grows the business.

Parents encourage behavioural attributes that creates a positively strong person.

God does the same.

Then behavioural attributes are God centred, the person is loved by both man and God.

In relationships, at home, in marriages, it is these God centred behavioural attributes that create lasting bonds of love and respect.

In God Alone

When we use our minds and our bodies, in Godly fashion, then we develop excellent attitude.

Excellent attitude is profitable.

A God fearing woman, will, of necessity, spend time alone with God for the benefit of her household.

She will seek to make sure her children and her husband eat, she is not pushed or persuaded, she does so willingly with her hands.

The Bible says to us – seek and you will find. It is so sure – if you seek you will find. There is no time frame, there are no geographic bounds – it's all so open and open ended.

Only we, can limit ourselves.

Our attitude is what limits us – attitude about God, attitude about others, attitude about ourselves.

Nothing comes for free or falls from heaven. If anything does, we should run away, unless we can explain it.

When Solomon says in **Proverbs 31:13** *She seeketh wool, and flax, and worketh willingly with her hands,* he loaded that virtuous proverb statement - willing.

Solomon could have said she seeks oranges and lemons, or cabbages and tomatoes or *sadza* (corn/maize meal) *ne nyama* (and beef/chicken), but he did not.

Solomon talks substance. The things that matter.

A woman with Godly attitude thinks beyond the present and the immediate future. She thinks long term.

She does not think simple and easy, she thinks stability, and she thinks strength and dignity.

She is objective and fair minded. She is not an introvert, shying away from the things that matter, or burying her head in the sand.

She is a jerked up person. The person God is proud of, that society is proud of, regardless of negative sayers.

She is the person her children will call blessed.

To get wool you may need to start with shepherding the sheep and to get flax you may start with tilling the ground.

My view of a woman with an excellent attitude is Ruth, the Moabite.

Ruth knew what she wanted and determinedly went full steam ahead.

Invariably, when she did not know exactly what to do and when, she was willing to listen and learn.

She Is Clothed With Strength And Dignity and Laughs Without Fear Of The Future

She did not look to circumstance, but knew there was something better in life than her situation dictated then.

Ruth knew who to follow.

The Bible says

Now it came to pass in the days when the judges ruled, that there was a famine in the land. And a certain man of Bethlehemjudah went to sojourn in the country of Moab, he, and his wife, and his two sons.

2 And the name of the man was Elimelech, and the name of his wife Naomi, and the name of his two sons Mahlon and Chilion, Ephrathites of Bethlehemjudah. And they came into the country of Moab, and continued there **[Ruth 1-4].**

This Ruth narrative relates to the time Israel was governed by Judges.

At this time there was hardship in Israel from famine.

Times of famine not easy. Famine can challenge one's values and beliefs.

Famine tests who we are. Famine times are crises times with much wider ramifications.

It was not surprising then that this family of Elimelech went to Moab during this time of famine.

Moab was a land of Israel's "bad" cousins.

The decision to go to Moab was not easy. Going to Moab was a sign of hopelessness.

To Elimelech, Moab was the best alternative.

Crises demand that man think of or about consequence.

In crises man ought to keep the faith.

In crises man ought to wait upon the Lord.

In crises man ought to keep trusting, keep believing.

In crises man ought to remember that bad situations do not justify bad decisions.

Crises make one forget even standard procedure, or the basic about life.

Crises make you forget the simple.

It is in times of crises that attitude is manifest.

When tough times come, reason falters.

In crises, (even if it were ever possible to leave God), one needs God more.

Wholesome decision making is only possible in God.

Whilst God gives excellent attitude, excellency is defined or measured by or in crisis.

In God Alone

The good that came out of this trip done by impatient Israelites was Ruth, and God made everything good in His time.

God is merciful, when you keep at the ropes, He will restore!

³ And Elimelech Naomi's husband died; and she was left, and her two sons.

⁴ And they took them wives of the women of Moab; the name of the one was Orpah, and the name of the other Ruth: and they dwelled there about ten years.

⁵ And Mahlon and Chilion died also both of them; and the woman was left of her two sons and her husband.

Before Elimelech died, he and Naomi had gotten wives for their sons.

Ten years after landing in Moab things had really changed. Naomi had no husband and no sons.

For some, ten years is long, especially when things are bad – life tends to move very slowly. For others it's too short.

Whatever the situation, how you read time depends on one's situation.

⁶ Then she arose with her daughters in law, that she might return from the country of Moab: for she had heard in the country of Moab how that the LORD had visited his people in giving them bread.

⁷ Wherefore she went forth out of the place where she was, and her two daughters in law with her; and they went on the way to return unto the land of Judah.

Whatever our situation or circumstance, we ought to know *when* it's time to move.

A sulky attitude towards life does not give one perspective – it shrouds one's brain.

Thank God, Naomi knew Moab was not her country.

It had been wrong for Naomi to go there in the first place.

God remembers Naomi, even after losing everything she had had.

Life will happen. When God is with us, we will know how and where to go.

When life happens, we will go back to the father, back to our God.

The Bible says *⁸ And Naomi said unto her two daughters in law, Go, return each to her mother's house: the LORD deal kindly with you, as ye have dealt with the dead, and with me.*

⁹ *The LORD grant you that ye may find rest, each of you in the house of her husband. Then she kissed them; and they lifted up their voice, and wept.*

¹⁰ *And they said unto her, Surely we will return with thee unto thy people.*

¹¹ *And Naomi said, Turn again, my daughters: why will ye go with me? are there yet any more sons in my womb, that they may be your husbands?*

¹² *Turn again, my daughters, go your way; for I am too old to have an husband. If I should say, I have hope, if I should have an husband also to night, and should also bear sons;*

¹³ *Would ye tarry for them till they were grown? would ye stay for them from having husbands? nay, my daughters; for it grieveth me much for your sakes that the hand of the LORD is gone out against me.*

Emotional scene. Two young ladies clutching on to their mother in law.

This is typical of returning, especially when you now return with foreign goods.

When one returns, one needs to make certain declarations. When one returns, there is change of territory.

Naomi now had two people that did not belong to her own. She needed to let go and they would not let her.

I fail to imagine what would have happened if Orpah had chosen to take the trip to Bethlehem instead of Ruth.

Thank God it was Ruth that came. Thank God Orpah did not go with Naomi.

The Bible says,

14 And they lifted up their voice, and wept again: and Orpah kissed her mother in law; but Ruth clave unto her.

Both Ruth and Orpah had been married by brothers, had same mother in law, same circumstances, same situations.

Ruth and Orpah worshipped the same gods, they both heard their mother in law's words at the same time, they both cried.

Ruth and Orpah were in exactly the same situation.

However, their cries did not mean the same, Naomi's words did not carry the same weight or meaning, to Ruth and Orpah.

The difference was in their attitude. One's approach to life, one's outlook on what goes on, is their attitude.

That outlook, that approach, is based on one's faith, one's belief, one's thinking process.

Whatever seemed common between Ruth and Orpah was challenged when crisis came.

Each rested on what they believed, their gods.

When challenging times come, we all go back to our gods.

Naomi had to say this to Ruth,

15 Behold, thy sister in law is gone back unto her people, and unto her gods: return thou after thy sister in law.

Naomi could not have put it any better. She said to Ruth, your sister has gone to her people and her gods.

This is profound.

What people and what gods?

Ruth had decided.

My thinking is, Ruth did not make a decision then, Ruth had made a decision well before.

Ruth had committed to "fly together" with Naomi.

In the same way, Orpah had also committed, well before this day.

16 And Ruth said, Intreat me not to leave thee, or to return from following after thee: for whither thou goest, I will go;

and where thou lodgest, I will lodge· thy people shall be my people, and thy God my God:

How could Ruth let go of Naomi's God. Ruth was following Naomi's God.

Ruth was not following Naomi the mother in law. Ruth wanted to know more of the God of Israel, Naomi's God.

Naomi had nothing. No husband, no son, no bread. She had left her family more than a decade earlier and was probably forgotten by her own people.

Naomi must have been hesitant She did not know if she would be accepted back into the fold.

How could they remember one who had decided to go to Moab when things got challenging?

Why would anyone care whatever happened to Naomi in Moab?

To Ruth, Naomi could offer nothing that could be seen or touched – but Naomi had talked about her God. The Lord God who hears and who sees.

Ruth had heard Naomi talk about her God, the Lord God who would say "come, let us reason together".

He, Ruth wanted to be her God. As long as she stayed in Moab, she would have gods and not God.

In God Alone

17 Where thou diest, will I die, and there will I be buried: the LORD do so to me, and more also, if ought but death part thee and me.

18 When she saw that she was stedfastly minded to go with her, then she left speaking unto her.

Ruth succeeded. Ruth's success came from being steadfast in what she believed about Naomi's God.

19 So they two went until they came to Bethlehem. And it came to pass, when they were come to Bethlehem, that all the city was moved about them, and they said, Is this Naomi?

Naomi had changed. Not only had she lost what she had gone away with, but she had gained a daughter – loving and true – with excellent attitude.

20 And she said unto them, Call me not Naomi, call me Mara: for the Almighty hath dealt very bitterly with me.

21 I went out full and the LORD hath brought me home again empty: why then call ye me Naomi, seeing the LORD hath testified against me, and the Almighty hath afflicted me?

Not so Naomi! The Lord wanted to empty Naomi first so she could see God's onward provision.

22 So Naomi returned, and Ruth the Moabites, her daughter in law, with her, which returned out of the country of Moab: and they came to Bethlehem in the beginning of barley harvest.

She Is Clothed With Strength And Dignity and Laughs Without Fear Of The Future

2 *And Naomi had a kinsman of her husband's, a mighty man of wealth, of the family of Elimelech; and his name was Boaz.*

² *And Ruth the Moabitess said unto Naomi, Let me now go to the field, and glean ears of corn after him in whose sight I shall find grace. And she said unto her, Go, my daughter.*

What a relationship – God's mercies after Naomi's loss. God's mercies are new in everyone's morning.

³ *And she went, and came, and gleaned in the field after the reapers: and her hap was to light on a part of the field belonging unto Boaz, who was of the kindred of Elimelech.*

⁴ *And, behold, Boaz came from Bethlehem, and said unto the reapers, The LORD be with you. And they answered him, The LORD bless thee.*

The language was different. Greetings were in the name of the Lord.

⁵ *Then said Boaz unto his servant that was set over the reapers, Whose damsel is this?*

Identity is everything. When one does not belong, then that person is lost.

⁶ *And the servant that was set over the reapers answered and said, It is the Moabitish damsel that came back with Naomi out of the country of Moab:*

Associations matter. They build a person.

⁷ And she said, I pray you, let me glean and gather after the reapers among the sheaves: so she came, and hath continued even from the morning until now, that she tarried a little in the house.

What one does and how they do it is important.

⁸ Then said Boaz unto Ruth, Hearest thou not, my daughter? Go not to glean in another field, neither go from hence, but abide here fast by my maidens:

Mind who calls you his daughter?

⁹ Let thine eyes be on the field that they do reap, and go thou after them: have I not charged the young men that they shall not touch thee? and when thou art athirst, go unto the vessels, and drink of that which the young men have drawn.

Character speaks.

¹⁰ Then she fell on her face, and bowed herself to the ground, and said unto him, why have I found grace in thine eyes, that thou shouldest take knowledge of me, seeing I am a stranger?

God on our side, that is grace.

¹¹ And Boaz answered and said unto her, It hath fully been shewed me, all that thou hast done unto thy mother in law since the death of thine husband: and how thou hast left thy father and thy mother, and the land of thy nativity, and art come unto a people which thou knewest not heretofore.

¹² The LORD recompense thy work, and a full reward be given thee of the LORD God of Israel, under whose wings thou art come to trust.

An excellent attitude is rewarded excellently, by God.

To Ruth, Boaz is simply saying – I like what you do and how you do it.

That, is attitude.

It's not how we look that matters; it's how we relate that is seen!

The narrative of chapter 3 is a reflection of what God does to those that fear Him.

Both mother in law and daughter in law have one thing in common – they have left Moab and its gods.

³Then Naomi her mother in law said unto her, My daughter…

³Wash thyself therefore, and anoint thee, and put thy raiment upon thee, and get thee down to the floor: but make not thyself known unto the man, until he shall have done eating and drinking.

The labour of love – it shall always be greatly rewarded.

Naomi appreciated Ruth through and through.

She Is Clothed With Strength And Dignity and Laughs Without Fear Of The Future

Naomi had the experience, understood how things were done in Israel, and rose up to meet the challenges for her daughter in law.

4 And it shall be, when he lieth down, that thou shalt mark the place where he shall lie, and thou shalt go in, and uncover his feet, and lay thee down; and he will tell thee what thou shalt do.

5 And she said unto her, All that thou sayest unto me I will do.

Ruth did not doubt the intentions of her mother in law.

Ruth and Naomi were genuine; Moab was behind them.

6 And she went down unto the floor, and did according to all that her mother in law bade her.

7 And when Boaz had eaten and drunk, and his heart was merry, he went to lie down at the end of the heap of corn: and she came softly, and uncovered his feet, and laid her down.

8 And it came to pass at midnight, that the man was afraid, and turned himself: and, behold, a woman lay at his feet.

9 And he said, Who art thou? And she answered, I am Ruth thine handmaid: spread therefore thy skirt over thine handmaid; for thou art a near kinsman.

She Is Clothed With Strength And Dignity and Laughs Without Fear Of The Future

¹⁰ *And he said, Blessed be thou of the LORD, my daughter: for thou hast shewed more kindness in the latter end than at the beginning, inasmuch as thou followedst not young men, whether poor or rich.*

Awesome!

¹¹ *And now, my daughter, fear not; I will do to thee all that thou requirest: for all the city of my people doth know that thou art a virtuous woman.*

Virtue can never be hidden.

¹² *And now it is true that I am thy near kinsman: howbeit there is a kinsman nearer than I.*

¹³ *Tarry this night, and it shall be in the morning, that if he will perform unto thee the part of a kinsman, well; let him do the kinsman's part: but if he will not do the part of a kinsman to thee, then will I do the part of a kinsman to thee, as the LORD liveth: lie down until the morning.*

Goodness does not rush, because it is Godly.

¹⁷ *And she said, These six measures of barley gave he me; for he said to me, Go not empty unto thy mother in law.*

¹⁸ *Then said she, Sit still, my daughter, until thou know how the matter will fall: for the man will not be in rest, until he have finished the thing this day.*

Honour begets honour.

She Is Clothed With Strength And Dignity and Laughs Without Fear Of The Future

9 And Boaz said unto the elders, and unto all the people, Ye are witnesses this day, that I have bought all that was Elimelech's, and all that was Chilion's and Mahlon's, of the hand of Naomi.

10 Moreover Ruth the Moabitess, the wife of Mahlon, have I purchased to be my wife, to raise up the name of the dead upon his inheritance, that the name of the dead be not cut off from among his brethren, and from the gate of his place: ye are witnesses this day.

11 And all the people that were in the gate, and the elders, said, We are witnesses. The LORD make the woman that is come into thine house like Rachel and like Leah, which two did build the house of Israel: and do thou worthily in Ephratah, and be famous in Bethlehem:

God signed up the honourable into His eternal plans.

13 So Boaz took Ruth, and she was his wife.., the LORD gave her conception, and she bare a son.

14 And the women said unto Naomi, Blessed be the LORD, which hath not left thee this day without a kinsman, that his name may be famous in Israel.

15 And he shall be unto thee a restorer of thy life, and a nourisher of thine old age: for thy daughter in law, which loveth thee, which is better to thee than seven sons, hath born him.

God builds an attitude that is fit for heaven.

17 And the women her neighbours gave it a name, saying, There is a son born to Naomi; and they called his name Obed: he is the father of Jesse, the father of David.

Honour is not easily endowed;

Honour comes from admirable,

Honour comes from worthy,

Honour comes from praiseworthy,

Honour comes from morality,

Honour comes from principle,

Honour comes from goodness,

Honour comes from respect,

Honour comes from uprightness,

Honour comes from God.

STEP 5

OPEN MINDED

Open means giving access, it means exposure, open gives vision.

Open means other people can see through you.

The mind is often the one that blocks one from being open.

The mind can create barriers, by race, by gender, by age, by education, by geography, by any.

Open minded is a willingness to consider new ideas. It is being unprejudiced.

It is being impartial, fair, neutral and tolerant.

It is being balanced and objective.

Open minded ness, in a way, gives the other the benefit of the doubt.

Open minded means

A prudent woman should be as open minded as the open seas.

Open seas are able to carry all types of vessels, from the dry cargo ships to tugs.

The Lord God Almighty in His wisdom gave us capacity to do so, not as a punishing assignment but as a wholesome purpose driven life.

It is easier for a woman to make a difference, in families and in communities. This is true from Adam's Eve, through Abraham's Sarah, Joseph's Mary, from Jericho's Rachab to Magdala's Mary.

That life, that purposeful living, is only possible when the woman spends time – alone with God.

Not only will that woman, that spends time alone with God, be able to accommodate the vessels, she herself ought to be the vessel – that fits all situations of life.

A woman who spends time *alone* with God can be the dry cargo ship and she can be the tug – she can also be everything in between.

Life in itself is not one dimensional – it is very much multi-dimensional.

Life comes in all shapes and sizes, in every weight from grams to tonnes. That is why Solomon said

She is like the merchants' ships; she bringeth her food from afar **[Proverbs 31:14]**.

During Solomon's time, merchant ships were all strong, today's ships are stronger.

In God Alone

Today's woman, like today's merchant ship, is stronger.

She is a Ruth and an Esther, a Dorcas and a Lydia, she is a Deborah, she is the new vessel, modelled on the old, but just stronger, more enduring.

With God, she is the super vessel.

Large ships cannot trade on shallow waters – they need wide open seas.

Open minded women can do wonders – their shoulders are not soft; their muscles are stronger than the waves that beat them at sea.

Open seas are open – the sardines and the blue wales co-exist. There is plenty in a woman's life that can co-exist. Wifely duties, motherly duties, nurse tasks, gardener tasks, professional careers, town and country mix.

Not only does capacity exist in a woman to execute all, but she can do a lot at the same time. Women can multi task

Whilst at it, the woman should never lose sight of the fact that the icebergs and the reefs stay hidden out of sight in the day to day business – but both are terribly dangerous.

She Is Clothed With Strength And Dignity and Laughs Without Fear Of The Future

In God Alone

The narrative below, quoted as is, depicts the various merchant or cargo ships and the waters they float in.

In this narrative, words and sentences in bold highlight the learning aspects of the particular ship as it relates to world handlers – women.

The bulleted points are my analogy aspects.

As each category of ships is explained, first as a quality of ship and then the nature of its cargo, the purpose of this analysis is that each woman can relate to a particular vessel or combination of vessels.

This analogy will create a higher level of understanding of the fact that it is folly to start loading without creating time for God.

Without God, the journey of life will be perilous and unenjoyable.

Enjoy this tour!

'Modern seagoing commercial vessels **come in all shapes and sizes and are designed to carry a wide variety of cargoes.** This article will attempt to provide a brief overview of the main types that are plying the oceans today and give some history as to how each design has evolved.

To begin, the main cargo types should be defined. For the purposes of this article, cargoes shall be divided

---

She Is Clothed With Strength And Dignity and Laughs Without Fear Of The Future

into dry, liquid and specialised, with each of these divided further into sub categories. Dry cargoes include bulk, general and break-bulk, containers, reefer and Ro-Ro. Liquid cargoes are predominantly oil based but may also include chemicals and liquefied gasses. Specialised cargoes include passengers, livestock and heavy-lift/project.

- Each merchant ship knows its capacity – when and how it can break. Every woman should know her strength, and her weaknesses.
- Women ought to have self-awareness.

Dry Cargo Ships:

Historically, dry cargo vessels were the mainstay of the world's merchant fleet. Known as general cargo vessels, they would be "geared", that is **equipped with their own cargo loading equipment**, usually in the form of derricks. The cargo would be stowed in different holds and the speed and effectiveness of the loading/unloading process would depend on the skill of the ship's crew and the port workers or "Stevedores". Such ships would sometimes **operate a regular service** between two or more ports as "liners", **but could also operate in the "tramp trade" where vessels would go wherever they were required.**

- Most women are general cargo vessels. Most are not privy to what most men have access to, nor are they privileged in any significant way.

- The typical woman is in this category. She is expected to carry anything and everything.
- Everyone else expects the woman to deliver, regardless.
- In this environment, the best every woman can do is to make sure she develops her own specific and user-friendly loading equipment.
- No one will do the loading for us women. The loading is the most challenging part. The shoulders may fail to sustain the load.
- Offloading is easy. With experience, anyone can off load.
- Some of the cargo we carry is so dry, devoid of any feeling or good temperament.
- With God, any woman can carry her cargo. She can start the journey and finish it.
- With God, a woman has wisdom to select which cargo to carry.

Bulk Carriers:

For **dry cargoes with a high weight** to cost ratio such as coal, grain and ore, **economies of scale have produced the modern bulk carrier.** These usually large vessels are divided up into several separate holds covered by hatches. In port, cargo is loaded by conveyor and spouts or by crane and grab. Some bulk carriers are geared (usually a crane is located between each hatch) to allow the loading and unloading of cargo at berths without the need for shore equipment.

- A woman ought to know how to carry bulk.
- Women touch lives every day, from the baby in the crib to the lady or gentleman in the wheel chair.
- Women have staying power.
- Women, with grace from spending time alone with God, can bring dry cargo with high weight to shore.

For unloading, cranes with grabs are the norm although specialised equipment may be used for certain cargoes. **When vessels unload using cranes and grabs, personnel and vehicles will often be placed inside the holds to assist the process.** Cargo will usually be unloaded into hoppers and will then be transferred by conveyor to silos or open storage, smaller vessels may discharge directly into road vehicles.

- At times, women are expected to offload on their own, no cranes, no conveyor belts, no cars, and no people to assist.
- Resting on God, the burden bearer, women can deliver their bulk with ease.

General Cargo Vessels:

Although largely replaced by bulk and container carriers, general cargo vessels still operate throughout the world. **Cargo is usually in the form of pallets or bags and is known as break-bulk.** There may be specialised handling facilities for such cargo, but usually loading and unloading is carried out using cranes and straps (for boxes) or slings (for bags). **Loose or irregular cargo is also carried,** in this case the vessel's crew and port stevedores will **pack the cargo to minimise damage and maximise the utilisation of space**.

- Cargo carried by women is multi-dimensional. At times there is just no relationship in what a woman carried during an eight-hour working day.
- Regardless, women are expected to minimise damage and maximise the utilisation of space.
- God takes us women, through missions impossible!

Container Vessels:

Containers have become the main way of transporting manufactured goods around the world. **A container can be transferred between truck, train and ship relatively easily and is a standard size to simplify transportation. Containers can accommodate anything from foodstuffs to electrical equipment to automobiles.** Containers are also used to transport bagged and palletised goods, liquids and refrigerated cargo.

Standard containers are measured as TEUs (Twenty-foot Equivalent Units) and are generally 20 feet (1 TEU) or 40 feet (2 TEUs) long. All standard shipping containers are 8 feet wide and 8 feet 6 inches tall. **There are also longer, taller and even shorter standard sizes**, but these are less common.

Container ships are made up of several holds, each equipped with "cell guides" which allow the containers to slot into place. Once the first layers of containers have been loaded and the hatches closed, extra layers are loaded on top of the hatches. **Each container is then lashed to the vessel but also to each other to provide integrity**. Containers are usually loaded by specialised cranes or even general-purpose cranes with container lifting attachments but some small container vessels are geared to allow self-loading/discharging.

Container vessels are used predominantly on liner routes and are some of the biggest vessels afloat. Ultra Large Container Vessels (ULCVs) such as the Emma

Maersk (lead ship of the Maersk E-Class vessels) are able to carry approximately 15,000 TEU (depending on container weight). **Large container vessels are restricted by their size to certain ports around the world and are also unable to transit certain areas due to draft or, in the case of canals beam, restrictions.**

- Containerisation is an art. A woman ought to be able to put everything in context, in perspective.
- Containers carry anything and everything, from larger ships' component parts to toothpicks and needles.
- Containerisation is a smart process. One is avoiding mixing issues and tissues.
- Long haul and short haul goods are contained at different parts of the vessel.
- An anyhow woman cannot endure the process. A woman who spends time with God knows how to pack within the container and on deck.
- The art of containerisation makes the journey more rewarding.
- God, in **Proverbs 4:7** says

    Wisdom is the principal thing; therefore get wisdom: and with all thy getting get understanding."

In God Alone

Reefer Vessels:

Ships **designed to carry a refrigerated cargo usually comprising perishable goods** such as fruit or meats are known as "Reefer Vessels". **Cargo is stowed in holds which are then sealed and temperature controlled.** Traditional reefer vessels have been largely replaced by the use of reefer containers which may be carried on board a container vessel. **Reefer containers only need a power source to function** although they are usually loaded to allow the crew to inspect them during the voyage.

- Reefers are interesting. They are actually designed to carry refrigerated cargo.
- Refrigerated cargo can be quite demanding.
- Refrigerated cargo need specific temperatures.
- Refrigerated cargo can be quite "picky" when temperatures charge.
- Refrigerated cargo is sensitive cargo.
- Refrigerated cargo needs a power source to function. The cargo of this vessel cannot last without a power source.
- With refrigerated cargo, the carrier is kept on their toes
- The cargo cannot stand heat or the sun.
- Refrigerated cargo needs the Sun of righteousness, to keep the temperatures down.

She Is Clothed With Strength And Dignity and Laughs Without Fear Of The Future

Ro-Ro Vessels:

Roll on-Roll off or Ro-Ro vessels come in many forms including vehicle ferries and cargo ships carrying **truck trailers** but the major type used for the transport of road vehicles is the **car carrier**. These slab-sided vessels feature multiple vehicle decks comprising **parking lanes**, linked by internal ramps with access to the shore provided by one or more loading ramp. Cargo **capacity of such vessels is measured in Car Equivalent Units (CEU)** and the largest car carriers afloat today have a capacity of over 6,000 CEU.

- This is a huge vessel. This vessel carries heavy duty. It carries carriers! This is huge.

In God Alone

- Cargo is not measured in ordinary ways. Capacity is in Car Equivalent Units. What a vessel.
- Women are built for this type of cargo. No man can measure what and how women can endure.
- Only God knows how He structured women. The weight and the volume we carry is inconceivable.

Liquid Cargo Ships:

These vessels, collectively known as tankers, carry **a range of liquid cargoes.** Tankers were first developed in the mid nineteenth century when the use of iron allowed liquids to be carried in bulk **economically and without leakage**. Like the case of the bulk carrier, economies of scale have driven up the size of tankers and today the largest examples have a carrying capacity or "deadweight" of over 400,000 tons.

Tankers are divided into separate tanks into which the cargo is pumped via a pipeline system. Modern tankers have large and segregated ballast tanks to **allow them to sit lower in the water on the return 'empty' journey to improve stability**. Many tankers **also feature systems to add an inert gas to the tanks to reduce the risk of fire and explosion.**

- To carry a range of liquids, a woman has to continually "reinvent" themselves.

She Is Clothed With Strength And Dignity and Laughs Without Fear Of The Future

- To carry the liquid economically and without leakage seem to be contradictory. Economic is cheap. Delivery without leakage is expensive.
- The woman is expected to be able to deliver on both parameters.
- A woman's journey often has empty trips. Women often are physically and emotionally exhausted.
- God can give stability during those "empty" trips.
- Should life cause a fire and explodes, women who do spend time with God will not implode. These women will not collapse, they will not fail, crash.
- In God, these women will not shrink or break down.

Crude Carriers:

She Is Clothed With Strength And Dignity and Laughs Without Fear Of The Future

The largest ships afloat are the Very Large Crude Carriers (VLCCs) and the Ultra Large Crude Carriers (ULCCs). These ships are **designed to load crude oil and transport it to refineries around the world where it can be processed into petroleum products.** The largest crude carriers often load and unload at offshore buoys and terminals as they are too large to enter most ports.

- Crude carriers are amazing. Anything that is crude is offensive or coarse.
- Yes, coarse. At times, women are required to carry this cargo and take it to a refinery.
- This is awesome. God has made women true treasures in earthen vessels. At the end of the refining process, when the cargo is now petroleum jelly, there may be very little, if any, recognition for the crude carrier's role
- Man and man relationships need crude carriers to take the coarse back to God.

Product Carriers:

These vessels, which are generally **smaller than crude carriers, transport the refined products** from larger terminals to smaller ports around the world. Products carried can include petroleum, jet fuel, diesel, asphalt, lubricating oil and tar. Smaller tankers are also used to transport non-petroleum bulk liquids such as molasses and palm oil.

- Product carriers *seem* to have a lighter job, carrying what has already been processed.
- Product carriers carry what has been refined. Seems simple.
- Not so simple. Products are required by everyone. A product carrier has no rest.
- Product carriers travel to all sorts of ports, large and small.
- Products are required for delivery during specific time frames.
- Product carriers are supposed to be clean, efficient, articulate and time conscious.
- Product carriers know what it takes, and that is, only God perfects.

Chemical Carriers:

These ships usually have deadweight of 5,000-40,000 tons and often **have specialised cargo systems suited to the type of cargo carried. These systems can include heating or cooling apparatus and advanced cleaning systems to ensure the purity of a cargo is maintained when loaded into a tank that may have previously carried something different.**

- This is special, because chemicals are flammable, in most instances.
- The vessel's cargo is specialised, and so are its cargo carrying systems.

- From day one, even before loading, one already knows they are on a perilous journey.
- Should systems fail, then life is lost. Before life is lost, the pain of burning, as science says, is sore.
- God ought to lead that journey, should troubles arise, God heals all wounds.
- A woman ought to understand her particular environment; its nature, characteristics and level of heat resistance.
- Chemical reactions are often fatal, ranging from carbon to nuclear. Each woman ought to understand her operating environment and safety procedures.
- Chemicals can suck the oxygen out of the sea water. Without oxygen, there is no life. Without oxygen, one can simply not breathe.
- Chemical effect is long term. Outside God, a chemical effect will simply break women spirit.
- Chemical damage extends to the unborn. Offspring born after a chemical spill will be disadvantaged physically first, and then in every other respect.
- The specialised systems can include heating or cooling apparatus. Only God can keep the purity of the cargo.
- The system needs advanced cleaning systems

- Care should be taken to ensure there is no contamination with old and expired cargo.
- Only God can keep the purity of the cargo.

Liquefied Gas Carriers:

These ships began as **converted oil tankers but have evolved into highly specialised purpose-built vessels**. Designed to **carry Liquefied** Petroleum Gas (LPG) or Liquefied Natural Gas (LNG) **under pressure**,

the **cargo tanks are generally spherical for strength.**

LNG carriers are usually larger than those carrying LPG, the largest LNG carriers are the 'Q-Flex' vessels with a gas capacity of up to 266,000 cubic metres.

- Wow. Spherical for strength.
- Woman to woman: when you see another woman carrying a certain posture, do not be

quick to charge, she may be "spherical" so that she is able to carry her load, her cargo.
- A woman sitting, standing or even bending, spherically, is simply under pressure.

Specialised Cargoes:

Most types of cargo could be considered as specialised due to the specific loading, unloading or stowage arrangements required. Many such cargoes are however, moved with such regularity and ease that the term 'specialised' takes on a new meaning. For the purpose of this article, it refers to **cargoes that are either difficult to categorise as dry or liquid, or to cargoes that are relatively difficult to handle.**

Passenger Vessels:

This category includes everything from 10-person foot ferries up to cruise ships able to carry over 6,000 passengers. **Perhaps the most specialised cargo of all, the needs and desires of passengers have driven the design of the modern ferries and cruise vessels.**

Ferries, **once seen as 'a means to an end'** for most, are now lavishly equipped with lounges, restaurants, shops and entertainment facilities – particularly when the ferry is on a relatively long route. The ships have got larger too…

Many cruise vessels were originally liners which were **sent to warmer climates during seasonal bad weather on their regular routes.**

Today, **cruise passengers demand and expect a wide range of facilities** including casinos, gymnasiums, shops, theatres, cinemas, pools, restaurants and bars. Passenger cargo is intriguing. They are supposed to be so diverse and on top of their game, every time, everywhere.

- Passenger vessels are expected to be failsafe – its people on board.
- Passenger vessels are expected to accommodate – day and night.
- Passenger vessels are expected to be close to perfection, because the diner can also cook!

Livestock Carriers:

These ships are often **converted from other types of vessel** and are equipped with pens for large numbers of animals. The **main considerations** during the transport of livestock are **adequate ventilation, food and water, but also the ability of the reception facilities at the destination port to handle the cargo**. Some livestock carriers are reported to be able to transport up to 120,000 sheep. A Common route for livestock carriers is Australia and New Zealand to the Middle East.

- At times, the cargo we carry, as women, is not people, it is livestock.
- With livestock, the carrier has to be fit to accommodate the physical nature of the animal, and its temperament.
- With livestock, there is no spirituality to talk about. It is all very physical.
- Livestock should simply not be expected to think, as people would.
- Carrying livestock, we all need God.

Heavy-lift/Project Cargo Vessels:

These, mostly purpose built, vessels specialise in the **transport of extremely heavy or bulky objects such as other ships and large industrial components**. Some heavy-lift vessels are equipped with high capacity cranes to load at ports without a heavy-lift capability. Other types are semi-submersible, which allows a cargo to be floated into position before the heavy-lift vessel de-ballasts to lift the cargo out of the water.

Notable occasions where semi-submersible heavy-lift vessels have been used are the return of RFA Sir Tristram to the UK following the Falklands conflict and the return of the USS Cole to the United States following the bombing in Aden. Heavy-lift vessels have **also transported offshore platforms from their construction site to the drilling site.**

Common project cargoes are wind turbine blades and towers, quay cranes and industrial machinery. Some project cargo vessels have been **adapted further to suit their role**. 'Jack up' vessels for example are **able to put down 'legs' to lift themselves out of the water**. This is commonly used by vessels installing offshore wind farms **where stability is required** during the placing of the turbine towers.

- This is a good vessel. It can stand on its own.
- The vessel is expected and should be able to put down 'legs' to lift itself out of the water.
- It is called where stability is required. It is not like the other vessels, it is very stable and assured.
- This vessel is expected and is able to carry other ships!
- This vessel is big, at heart and all. It is required where cargo is bulky and heavy.
- This vessel is needed where other types of vessels are likely to fail, because they are equipped to lift themselves out of the water.
- It is a fact of life, if you cannot lift yourself out of the water, you drown.

Tugs:

Even with the advent of highly manoeuvrable vessels equipped with thrusters and azimuth pods, the tug is still vitally important to the maritime industry.

Modern tugs are **highly manoeuvrable with pulling power** (bollard pull) sometimes in excess of 100 tonnes, although harbour tugs are generally much less powerful. Such vessels are **on hand** in ports around the world **to assist** in the berthing, unberthing and movement of large or less manoeuvrable vessels within port limits. Tugs are **also used to assist the most manoeuvrable vessels during periods of bad weather or when carrying dangerous or polluting cargoes.** Harbour tugs are also often employed to move barges, floating cranes and personnel around ports. **Larger units are kept on standby in strategic locations to act as deep-sea rescue and salvage tugs.**

Tugs are also used to tow barges from port to port; these sea-going tugs are also employed for the movement of large structures such as offshore platforms and floating storage units. Some tugs are utilised to push barges, this is particularly common on rivers where the **tug is able to exert more turning force** on the tow. There are also tugs that are designed to 'slot' into a barge or hull, once secured, this composite unit behaves and is treated like a standard powered vessel. These composite units, like tugs employed to push the cargo, are more common on North American river and coastal trade.

- I like the tugs. Always ready to lend a hand.

She Is Clothed With Strength And Dignity and Laughs Without Fear Of The Future

- All these ships described above, with all their amazing attributes, will always need the Tug vessel.
- That ability to help, to see where the need is, comes from our Almighty God.

Vessel-Types-Explained-
http://www.portinfo.co.uk/portinformation/
ourmaritimeblog/vessel-types-explained

When Solomon looked at the various vessels of the day, as he traded with many of his neighbours, he considered a prudent woman, is like a Merchant ship, by God's design, by God's inexhaustible grace.

Like any ship – a woman ought to know their cargo. Is it liquid which can spill easily, is it glass which breaks, is it a perishable?

No woman should compare their cargo with another's. The cargo is very different. The tonnage may be the same but the texture is different.

The journey to an off-loading bay may be shorter than the next ship of similar size.

The weather that shapes your route may be stormy when another has calm seas.

The prudent woman is the best vessel, a vessel of honour; a woman whose thinking, capacity, strength, and attitude can change life and world economies.

That woman cannot walk alone – she needs the infinite connection to heaven's infinite power source; only when she spends time alone, with God.

This is awesome. This lady cannot walk alone. She is incapable of walking alone.

Woman, let God take care of your journey, because only God can ride the rough seas we travel every moment of our time, whether loading, sailing or offloading.

Only God can manage the cargo we carry.

STEP 6

PROACTIVE FAR SIGHTEDNESS

The book of Proverbs gives serious intelligence gathering for women. The book of proverbs gives brain power.

Intelligence gathering is an aspect of life that we sometimes neglect, at our own peril.

Solomon says in **Proverbs 14:15.**

The simple believeth every word: but the prudent man looketh well to his going.

Man being mostly generic, in the words of Solomon, it is important to look at life squarely "in the eye".

When you do, when you reflect and introspect, you are wiser.

When you reflect, you also know, as hindsight often gives 20/20 vision.

However, for going forward positions, one needs to be pro-active, one needs to be far sighted, one need both.

When you look at life squarely, you get wisdom, you understand.

Looking gives knowledge.

For knowledge, for wisdom, for understanding, we need God.

The Lord knows the end from the beginning, for He lives from everlasting to everlasting.

Our Lord God, is the all-seeing God.

A woman who stays with God, always in prayer position, cannot be taken by surprise.

She has foresight, because the Lord God goes before her and with her.

She is proactive. She does not wait until all is clear – when the day has broken – to start acting.

Proactive and pre-emptive often mean the same in context. A proactive lady acts pre-emptively.

She does what she needs to do before the event, whilst the event comes with foresight.

She has so much wisdom she can literally "foretell" what is likely to happen.

And wisdom, comes from God. The Bible in the book of James says we can pray for wisdom.

Solomon says in **Proverbs 31:15**

She Is Clothed With Strength And Dignity and Laughs Without Fear Of The Future

She riseth also while it is yet night, and giveth meat to her household, and a portion to her maidens.

Proactive behaviour involves acting in advance of a future situation, rather than reacting.

It means taking control and making things happen rather than adjusting to a situation or waiting for something to happen.

In workplaces, proactive employees generally do not need to be asked to act, nor do they require detailed instructions.

The merits of proactiveness are best illustrated by the story of Rachab or Rahab in Joshua chapter 2.

As I read this passage of scripture, I made my own assessment of what probably transpired (in bold);

2 And Joshua the son of Nun sent out of Shittim two men to spy secretly, saying, Go view the land, even Jericho. And they went, and came into an harlot's house, named Rahab, and lodged there.

God is no respecter of persons – He uses anyone to accomplish His purpose.

² And it was told the king of Jericho, saying, Behold, there came men in hither to night of the children of Israel to search out the country.

In God Alone

Dance like the whole world is watching – who would have known the spy mission.

³ And the king of Jericho sent unto Rahab, saying, Bring forth the men that are come to thee, which are entered into thine house: for they be come to search out all the country.

⁴ And the woman took the two men, and hid them, and said thus, There came men unto me, but I wist not whence they were:

Sometimes, sometimes – we just do not know....

⁵ And it came to pass about the time of shutting of the gate, when it was dark, that the men went out: whither the men went I wot not: pursue after them quickly; for ye shall overtake them.

⁶ But she had brought them up to the roof of the house, and hid them with the stalks of flax, which she had laid in order upon the roof.

There are questions that we may never be able to answer – why and how.

Why and how did the Lord direct the spies to Rahab's house, why and how could she so understand this spy mission,

Did she really know the end game – was it just foresight?

She Is Clothed With Strength And Dignity and Laughs Without Fear Of The Future

⁷ And the men pursued after them the way to Jordan unto the fords: and as soon as they which pursued after them were gone out, they shut the gate.

It is the Lord's doing that our enemies "can pursue us" when we really haven't gone anywhere.

The Lord just makes sure we are fully covered by "stalks of flax" – covered by unexpected people in unexpected places – the roof of the house.

On the roof of the house, heaven sees us but earth does not.

At the roof of the house, only those that think like us, hear like us and see like us – would know. These are the collaborators of our faith!

⁸ And before they were laid down, she came up unto them upon the roof;

⁹ And she said unto the men, I know that the LORD hath given you the land, and that your terror is fallen upon us, and that all the inhabitants of the land faint because of you.

¹⁰ For we have heard how the LORD dried up the water of the Red sea for you, when ye came out of Egypt; and what ye did unto the two kings of the Amorites, that were on the other side Jordan, Sihon and Og, whom ye utterly destroyed.

¹¹ And as soon as we had heard these things, our hearts did melt, neither did there remain any more courage in any man, because of you: for the LORD your God, he is God in heaven above, and in earth beneath.

She knew – the prostitute knew – she says "I know".

The whole city of Jericho had heard what the God of Israel had done but Rahab *knew* the same God had given Israel the land.

Rahab had that kind of faith, regardless of what she was doing for "a living".

Rahab had discernment, judgement, understanding and foresight.

12 Now therefore, I pray you, swear unto me by the LORD, since I have shewed you kindness, that ye will also shew kindness unto my father's house, and give me a true token:

13 And that ye will save alive my father, and my mother, and my brethren, and my sisters, and all that they have, and deliver our lives from death.

Rahab was shrewd. She was not selfish. She was prudent.

14 And the men answered her, Our life for yours, if ye utter not this our business. And it shall be, when the LORD hath given us the land, that we will deal kindly and truly with thee.

Rahab was more convinced about the Lord having given the spies the land than the spies were.

The spies are thinking of a future time, in their when the Lord has given us the land".

Rahab is thinking, the Lord your God *has* given you the land!

15 Then she let them down by a cord through the window: for her house was upon the town wall, and she dwelt upon the wall.

16 And she said unto them, Get you to the mountain, lest the pursuers meet you; and hide yourselves there three days, until the pursuers be returned: and afterward may ye go your way.

Rahab knew three days in hiding was enough. Not too early to let go and not too late.

Rahab let herself be – she made conversation with God's people.

17 And the men said unto her, We will be blameless of this thine oath which thou hast made us swear.

18 Behold, when we come into the land, thou shalt bind this line of scarlet thread in the window which thou didst let us down by: and thou shalt bring thy father, and thy mother, and thy brethren, and all thy father s household, home unto thee.

19 And it shall be, that whosoever shall go out of the doors of thy house into the street, his blood shall be upon his head, and we will be guiltless: and whosoever shall be with thee in the house, his blood shall be on our head, if any hand be upon him.

²⁰ And if thou utter this our business, then we will be quit of thine oath which thou hast made us to swear.

The spies' faith went up as Rahab made conversation with them. Rahab made them swear – she was so sure.

The spies have Rahab a red rope (this line of scarlet).

Really – the spies had a red rope!

The spies did not ask Rahab to get a line of scarlet – they had a particular type – ***this*** *line of scarlet.*

What were spies doing with red things?

Rahab probably saw *that* line of scarlet, and she knew, this was the Lord's program.

Rahab had heard, perhaps not everything, but had heard something.

Rahab was quick to remember. How could she not?

There had been Eden, through to Egypt, now coming to Jericho.

Rahab knew, if you collaborate with this God, the God of the red rope, you would live.

That plan, that program needed one collaborator – one woman, Rahab.

She was famous, but for the wrong reasons. Yet, the Lord knew her name.

Those thousands of years, from creation to redemption, were in the sands and sand dunes of Canaan. There were some in the land that belonged to the faith – the collaborators of Israel and their God. They were to be roped in, in God's time.

[21] *And she said, According unto your words, so be it. And she sent them away, and they departed: and she bound the scarlet line in the window.*

Rahab had to do her part: bind the scarlet rope on her window.

The window belonged to Rahab, but the scarlet rope had been given her.

Rahab was careful not to replace *this* rope with hers – she understood this God was specific, and if she wanted delivery – it had to be *that* line of scarlet.

Rahab needed to get her household to come to her house. If they were in her house, the red rope would cover them. Outside, they would be lost.

One can imagine how Rahab felt when the Israelites started singing, seven days they sang. She knew it was not going to be for long. They in the house, needed to hold on.

Rahab must have re assured them – we have the red rope tied to our window. We shall be delivered!

²² *And they went, and came unto the mountain, and abode there three days, until the pursuers were returned: and the pursuers sought them throughout all the way, but found them not.*

²³ *So the two men returned, and descended from the mountain, and passed over, and came to Joshua the son of Nun, and told him all things that befell them:*

²⁴ *And they said unto Joshua, Truly the LORD hath delivered into our hands all the land; for even all the inhabitants of the country do faint because of us.*

Rahab gave life to her household, and bread to all that were with her, as they dwell in Israel even to this day.

Woman, it does not matter how you start, mind how you end.

STEP 7

HUGE SELF ESTEEM

How we value and perceive our self-worth is important.

Women who spend time with God have high regard of themselves; they have reverence, honour, approval, respect, admiration and appreciation of themselves.

They have huge self-esteem.

How you hold yourself – the face you put forward – of yourself, determines what and how you do what you ought to do.

There are women who cannot and will not do anything.

Not because they are any different from the next woman – but because they have a battered self-esteem.

These women allow anyone to infringe on their emotional space.

The careful and practical woman's huge self-esteem comes from

- o the knowledge that her help comes from the Lord, who made heaven and earth,

- being peaceful,
- being grateful,
- praising the Lord, in all circumstances and situations,
- being content. Life is not all about crowns and tiaras.
- the conviction that without God there is no life – everything simply fails to exist – our dreams, our aspirations, our everything.

This woman is grounded in her faith and can sing the song:

> I will lift up mine eyes to the hills
> From whence cometh my help,
> My help cometh from the Lord,
> The Lord which made Heaven and Earth.
>
> He said He would not suffer thy foot,
> Thy foot to be moved;
> The Lord which keepeth thee,
> He will not slumber nor sleep.
>
> Oh the Lord is thy keeper,
> The Lord is thy shade
> Upon thy right hand,
> Upon thy right hand.
>
> No, the sun shall not smite thee by day,
> Nor the moon by night,
> He shall preserve thy soul
> Even forever more.
>
> [Chorus]
> My help, my help, my help,

In God Alone

All of my help cometh from the Lord.

Oh the Lord is thy keeper
The Lord is thy shade
Upon thy right hand no the sun shall not smite thee
Any day nor the moon by night he shall preserve thy soul even for ever more
My help my help my help all of my help cometh from the Lord

The Brooklyn Tabernacle Choir

Solomon says in **Proverbs 31.16** this woman

Considereth a field, and buyeth it: with the fruit of her hands she planteth a vineyard.

When you think that the asset the whole Bible alludes to more than any other asset, is land – from the Garden of Eden, the journeys of Abraham and God's promises, the Israelites in Egypt, the captivity of Israel into Babylon, the promise of God through Jesus of redemption to a better land, Solomon's statement becomes very inspiring to this woman.

This woman, because she thinks of buying land and planting vineyards, she is really at the top of the ladder.

Ladies who spend time with God rarely think about pots and pans, plates and dishes, cups and saucers; they operate at a much higher level – of fields and vineyards!

She Is Clothed With Strength And Dignity and Laughs Without Fear Of The Future

In **Genesis 12:6** the Bible says

" Abram traveled through the land as far as the site of the great tree of Moreh at Shechem. At that time the Canaanites were in the land. ⁷ The LORD appeared to Abram and said, "To your offspring I will give this land".

This is huge. On creation, God created land and everything that thrives on land, and He saw that it was good.

Women are not lesser beings. Women can too, possess the land.

In **Genesis 15;7** God also said to Abraham,

"I am the LORD, who brought you out of Ur of the Chaldeans to give you this land to take possession of it."

Women can also transact, on land and for land.

In **Genesis 15:18** the Bible says

On that day the LORD made a covenant with Abram and said, "To your descendants I give this land, from the Wadi of Egypt to the great river, the Euphrates — ¹⁹ the land of the Kenites, Kenizzites, and Kadmonites, ²⁰ Hittites, Perizzites, Rephaites, ²¹ Amorites, and Canaanites, Girgashites and Jebusites."

In **Genesis 17:8** God says to Abraham

In God Alone

"The whole land of Canaan, where you now reside as a foreigner, I will give as an everlasting possession to you and your descendants after you; and I will be their God."

The Lord gave because His children could not be foreigners for ever. Being foreign meant being subordinate.

God's children could not be minor, inferior or secondary. Solomon recognizes that women cannot be either; because they are God's children.

That is why **1st John 3** says,

1behold, what manner of love the Father has bestowed upon us, that we should be called sons (and daughters) of God"

A child of God is a child of God, man or woman. If it was any different Jesus would have said – let all male children come to me...

Without land one will always be a foreigner – one has no power, no control, one cannot set the rules.

Without land, one has no identity, as a foreigner simply does not belong.

God left room for women to set boundaries and take charge. The foreigner mentality attaches to women who think small - hats and shoes, or skirts and blouses.

They think land is burdensome – how will they carry it when they are expected to move over!

Thinking land is thinking permanency. It is saying, am here too.

In **Genesis 28** the Bible says

¹So Isaac called for Jacob and blessed him. Then he commanded him: "Do not marry a Canaanite woman. ² Go at once to Paddan Aram, to the house of your mother's father Bethuel. Take a wife for yourself there, from among the daughters of Laban, your mother's brother. ³ May God Almighty bless you and make you fruitful and increase your numbers until you become a community of peoples. ⁴ May he give you and your descendants the blessing given to Abraham, so that you may take possession of the land where you now reside as a foreigner, the land God gave to Abraham."

In the land that the Lord gives, even women will become a community of peoples.

There are conditions, higher attributes and higher relationships that govern land and land issues, over and above the actual purchase of land.

A woman who buys land, therefore, operates at that higher level.

The scriptures quoted below highlight this concept: - God says in:

Jeremiah 27:5

- "It is I who by my great power and my outstretched arm have made the earth, with the men and animals that are on the earth, and I give it to whomever it seems right to me.

Psalm 119:45

- And I shall walk in a wide place, for I have sought your precepts.

Jeremiah 32:44

- Fields shall be bought for money, and deeds shall be signed and sealed and witnessed, in the land of Benjamin, in the places about Jerusalem, and in the cities of Judah, in the cities of the hill country, in the cities of the Shephelah, and in the cities of the Negeb; for I will restore their fortunes, declares the LORD."

Isaiah 65:21-22

- They shall build houses and inhabit them; they shall plant vineyards and eat their fruit. They shall not build and another inhabit; they shall not plant and another eat; for like the days of a tree shall the days of my people be, and my chosen shall long enjoy the work of their hands.

Matthew 6:33

- But seek first the kingdom of God and his righteousness, and all these things will be added to you.

Psalm 16:6
- The lines have fallen for me in pleasant places; indeed, I have a beautiful inheritance.

Numbers 14:8
- If the LORD delights in us, he will bring us into this land and give it to us, a land that flows with milk and honey.

Matthew 21:33-46
- "Hear another parable. There was a master of a house who planted a vineyard and put a fence around it and dug a winepress in it and built a tower and leased it to tenants, and went into another country. When the season for fruit drew near, he sent his servants to the tenants to get his fruit. And the tenants took his servants and beat one, killed another, and stoned another. Again, he sent other servants, more than the first. And they did the same to them. Finally, he sent his son to them, saying, 'They will respect my son.'

Jeremiah 29:7
- But seek the welfare of the city where I have sent you into exile, and pray to the LORD on its behalf, for in its welfare you will find your welfare.

Joshua 18:1-28

- *Then the whole congregation of the people of Israel assembled at Shiloh and set up the tent of meeting there. The land lay subdued before them. There remained among the people of Israel seven tribes whose inheritance had not yet been apportioned. So Joshua said to the people of Israel, "How long will you put off going in to take possession of the land, which the LORD, the God of your fathers, has given you? Provide three men from each tribe, and I will send them out that they may set out and go up and down the land. They shall write a description of it with a view to their inheritances, and then come to me. They shall divide it into seven portions. Judah shall continue in his territory on the south, and the house of Joseph shall continue in their territory on the north. ...*

Joshua 2:24

- *And they said to Joshua, "Truly the LORD has given all the land into our hands. And also, all the inhabitants of the land melt away because of us."*

Matthew 5:5

- *"Blessed are the meek, for they shall inherit the earth.*

This land issue is not small. It gives power to shovel, to move things.

Land gives control and influence

The details in **Jeremiah 32**, where God instructs Jeremiah to buy a piece of land are quite telling. The long and short of it is that God is involved in our everyday transactions – let alone in our land.

The Bible says" This *is the word that came to Jeremiah from the* LORD *in the tenth year of Zedekiah king of Judah, which was the eighteenth year of Nebuchadnezzar.* ² *The army of the king of Babylon was then besieging Jerusalem, and Jeremiah the prophet was confined in the courtyard of the guard in the royal palace of Judah.*

³ *Now Zedekiah king of Judah had imprisoned him there, saying, "Why do you prophesy as you do? You say, 'This is what the* LORD *says: I am about to give this city into the hands of the king of Babylon, and he will capture it.* ⁴ *Zedekiah king of Judah will not escape the Babylonians but will certainly be given into the hands of the king of Babylon, and will speak with him face to face and see him with his own eyes.* ⁵ *He will take Zedekiah to Babylon, where he will remain until I deal with him, declares the* LORD. *If you fight against the Babylonians, you will not succeed."*

⁶ *Jeremiah said, "The word of the* LORD *came to me:* ⁷ *Hanamel son of Shallum your uncle is going to come to you and say, 'Buy my field at Anathoth, because as nearest relative it is your right and duty to buy it.'*

⁸ *"Then, just as the* LORD *had said, my cousin Hanamel came to me in the courtyard of the guard and said, 'Buy my*

field at Anathoth in the territory of Benjamin. Since it is your right to redeem it and possess it, buy it for yourself.'

"I knew that this was the word of the LORD; ⁹ so I bought the field at Anathoth from my cousin Hanamel and weighed out for him seventeen shekels of silver. ¹⁰ I signed and sealed the deed, had it witnessed, and weighed out the silver on the scales. ¹¹ I took the deed of purchase — the sealed copy containing the terms and conditions, as well as the unsealed copy — ¹² and I gave this deed to Baruch son of Neriah, the son of Mahseiah, in the presence of my cousin Hanamel and of the witnesses who had signed the deed and of all the Jews sitting in the courtyard of the guard.

¹³ "In their presence I gave Baruch these instructions: ¹⁴ 'This is what the LORD Almighty, the God of Israel, says: Take these documents, both the sealed and unsealed copies of the deed of purchase, and put them in a clay jar so they will last a long time. ¹⁵ For this is what the LORD Almighty, the God of Israel, says: Houses, fields and vineyards will again be bought in this land.'

¹⁶ "After I had given the deed of purchase to Baruch son of Neriah, I prayed to the LORD:

¹⁷ "Ah, Sovereign LORD, you have made the heavens and the earth by your great power and outstretched arm. Nothing is too hard for you.

¹⁸ You show love to thousands but bring the punishment for the parents' sins into the laps of their children after them. Great and mighty God, whose name is the LORD Almighty,

¹⁹ great are your purposes and mighty are your deeds. Your eyes are open to the ways of all mankind; you reward each person according to their conduct and as their deeds deserve.

²⁰ You performed signs and wonders in Egypt and have continued them to this day, in Israel and among all mankind, and have gained the renown that is still yours. ²¹ You brought your people Israel out of Egypt with signs and wonders, by a mighty hand and an outstretched arm and with great terror.

²² You gave them this land you had sworn to give their ancestors, a land flowing with milk and honey. ²³ They came in and took possession of it, but they did not obey you or follow your law; they did not do what you commanded them to do. So you brought all this disaster on them.

²⁴ "See how the siege ramps are built up to take the city. Because of the sword, famine and plague, the city will be given into the hands of the Babylonians who are attacking it. What you said has happened, as you now see. ²⁵ And though the city will be given into the hands of the Babylonians, you, Sovereign LORD, say to me, 'Buy the field with silver and have the transaction witnessed.'"

The narration above has a myriad of doctrine and prophecy interpretation.

The more literal is – land is bought and sold by children of God.

Land has substance, land transactions are long term.

Buying land is a faith issue.

One cannot buy land if they do not believe.

I say, woman, buy your piece of land and have it witnessed.

It does not matter what is happening around you, houses and cities will be built.

Women that spend time with God do not just think, they act.

These women plant their vineyards on fields they bought!

They do not take what does not belong to them – the silver and the gold is the fruit of their hands.

God does not discriminate.

In 1st Chronicles, when God inspired His writers to tell the story of Israel, a line (in brackets) had to be added.

The line is **1 Chronicles 7:24**

And his daughter was Sherah, who built Bethhoron the nether, and the upper, and Uzzensherah.

This was a descendant of Ephraim, Joseph's son. She built two cities!

The all-important thing is, God ought to be in it.

If not, lands and fields we buy will not be productive, the vines will not bear fruit and the cities will not last.

That is why **Isaiah 5:8** says

Woe to you who add house to house, and join field to field till no space is left and you live alone in the land. ⁹ The LORD Almighty has declared in my hearing: "Surely the great houses will become desolate, the fine mansions left without occupants. ¹⁰ A ten-acre vineyard will produce only a bath of wine; a homer of seed will yield only an ephah of grain." and

Leviticus 25:23 also says,

²³ *'The land must not be sold permanently, because the land is mine and you reside in my land as foreigners and strangers.*

As the Psalmist would say in **Psalms 24:1** *The earth is the Lord's and the fullness therein.*

Land issues are directed by the Lord God Almighty.

Solomon says the woman he so adores, considers a field and buys it.

That woman ought to know God, as God.

When God is in the transaction, He will not only bless but protects. He knows all the incidents, all the conversations, and all the plans the enemy has over your field.

In the book **1 Kings 21**, God Himself directs victory over the battles fought over Naboth's Vineyard.

The Bible says; *sometime later there was an incident involving a vineyard belonging to Naboth the Jezreelite. The vineyard was in Jezreel, close to the palace of Ahab king of Samaria.* ² *Ahab said to Naboth, "Let me have your vineyard to use for a vegetable garden, since it is close to my palace. In exchange I will give you a better vineyard or, if you prefer, I will pay you whatever it is worth."*

³ *But Naboth replied, "The LORD forbid that I should give you the inheritance of my ancestors."*

⁴ *So Ahab went home, sullen and angry because Naboth the Jezreelite had said, "I will not give you the inheritance of my ancestors." He lay on his bed sulking and refused to eat.*

⁵ *His wife Jezebel came in and asked him, "Why are you so sullen? Why won't you eat?"*

⁶ *He answered her, "Because I said to Naboth the Jezreelite, 'Sell me your vineyard; or if you prefer, I will give you another vineyard in its place.' But he said, 'I will not give you my vineyard.'"*

⁷ *Jezebel his wife said, "Is this how you act as king over Israel? Get up and eat! Cheer up. I'll get you the vineyard of Naboth the Jezreelite."*

⁸ *So she wrote letters in Ahab's name, placed his seal on them, and sent them to the elders and nobles who lived in Naboth's city with him. ⁹ In those letters she wrote:*

"Proclaim a day of fasting and seat Naboth in a prominent place among the people. ¹⁰ But seat two scoundrels opposite him and have them bring charges that he has cursed both God and the king. Then take him out and stone him to death."

¹¹ *So the elders and nobles who lived in Naboth's city did as Jezebel directed in the letters she had written to them. ¹² They proclaimed a fast and seated Naboth in a prominent place among the people. ¹³ Then two scoundrels came and sat opposite him and brought charges against Naboth before the people, saying, "Naboth has cursed both God and the king." So they took him outside the city and stoned him to death.¹⁴ Then they sent word to Jezebel: "Naboth has been stoned to death."*

¹⁵ *As soon as Jezebel heard that Naboth had been stoned to death, she said to Ahab, "Get up and take possession of the vineyard of Naboth the Jezreelite that he refused to sell you. He is no longer alive, but dead."¹⁶ When Ahab heard that Naboth was dead, he got up and went down to take possession of Naboth's vineyard.*

¹⁷ *Then the word of the* LORD *came to Elijah the Tishbite: ¹⁸ "Go down to meet Ahab king of Israel, who rules in Samaria. He is now in Naboth's vineyard, where he has gone to take possession of it.*

She Is Clothed With Strength And Dignity and Laughs Without Fear Of The Future

The Bible says this issue was an incident – an episode in a long line of events!

The woman who buys land ought to be bold and assertive, not arrogant, not rude; she ought to be exceptional in all her doings.

This woman has to be prayerful.

Land issues are emotive. What is heartening is

- If the Lord God Almighty directed the transaction – set the boundaries of what is yours, the same Lord will let you know who walks in your field.
- Even when Naboth was dead, God still said the land belonged to Naboth.

Woman, when you buy your land, do not let it go – for silver or for gold. Do not exchange it for goods of lesser value.

It's not just about the physical land, it is about the higher Godly values.

We cannot walk the paths of this world and get there, unless the Lord walks with us, even as we consider buying our fields and planting our vineyards.

STEP 8

POSITIVE

Staying positive in this challenging world needs a lot of brain power.

The ability to think and put things into their proper perspective.

Positive women not only survive, they live.

Positive women do not easily get overwhelmed, in the face of adversity.

Adversity means hardship, difficulty, danger, misfortune, harsh conditions, and hard times. The opposite is privilege, honour, treat, pleasure, joy, source of pride, freedom, and license.

For most women, life is full of adversity. The weapon is positive thinking.

Positive means being optimistic, confident, constructive, helpful, encouraging, affirmative, progressive and up looking.

This type of environment – full of adversity, calls for a woman who Solomon says in

Proverbs 31:17 She *girdeth her loins with strength, and strengtheneth her arms.*

To being positive, there is no substitute.

Positive thinking is premised on the word of God, through prayer.

When we pray, we pour out our hearts to God, and claim God's promises on those that fear Him, trust Him and honour Him.

As we pray, we gird our loins with strength. Strength in every way – physical, spiritual, mental, all.

Girding is quite loaded; it is binding, restraining, fixing and tightening.

A woman's life is either of these on a daily basis. At one time it is binding wounded limbs of relatives, children, a spouse.

Wounded egos need to be bound, attitudes of relatives need to be bound, and childhood habits needs to be bound.

Egos are most significant – wounded or not.

Managing egos is managing a whole being – personalities, characters, selves, self-images, individualities and opinions of self.

These also vary not just from individual to individual, but season to season. Sometimes, some seasons are not in months, but in weeks and some in days.

Seasons can run into years.

Girding your loins with strength is an exercise of the fruit of the spirit – love, joy, peace and all.

This life does not support feeble mentality.

Sometimes binding requires prayer and fasting. You forget to bind at your own peril.

Solomon's women lived in a complex of more than one thousand wives and concubines – what a situation. This woman needed a lot of strength to survive.

Thank God, for survival is victory!

A woman's loin is anything from her belly button to her thighs. Why not the chest to the top of the head?

The chest is the heart area, and the head is the mind area, the senses are all over the body.

A woman's heart and mind will tell her what to do – but the doing needs grit – perseverance, determination and bravery.

The brain can give you logic, but a bound loin will give you perseverance. Simple tasks like collecting firewood in the rural areas, fetching water from rivers, sweeping the yard, bathing the children and laundry – can leave you hard and dry.

Your mind will record "tired", but a strengthened loin will say not yet – I can do a little more.

Caring for the sick and raising children can be overwhelming, but a strengthened loin will, with calmness endure.

Life demands arms that are strong.

Prayer strengthens our arms. The Psalmist says in **Psalms 18:39**

"For thou hast girded me with strength unto the battle: thou hast subdued under me those that rose up against me."

This is what prayer does. Being alone with God ceases to be an option.

Life is a fight. We fight enemies of poverty, of disease and we fight adversaries.

The Bible also says in **Isaiah 41:10**

"Fear thou not; for I am with thee: be not dismayed; for I am thy God: I will strengthen thee; yea, I will help thee; yea, I will uphold thee with the right hand of my righteousness."

This assurance reinforces the fact that without strengthened arms we are in trouble.

Solomon says in **Proverbs 10:4** *Lazy hands make for poverty, but diligent hands bring wealth.*

Lazy hands are idle hands, sluggish and slothful. No one wants to stay or live with anyone whose hands are so defined. Either they do not want to start doing anything at all, or when they do, they are sluggish and slothful.

A woman's hands should be energetic. Nothing falls from the sky – if it does, all will run away.

The result of lazy hands is poverty.

The owner of lazy hands still wants to eat and sleep on a good bed. The mind of same expects someone will provide. The owner of such hands is a challenge to all around.

But diligent hands bring wealth. Diligent is hardworking, industrious, meticulous, conscientious, thorough and attentive.

Lazy hands and diligent hands cannot live together – it's a sure source of conflict.

In **Proverbs 13:4** Solomon says *A sluggard's appetite is never filled, but the desires of the diligent are fully satisfied.*

It is no brainer that a sluggish person (sluggard) has a huge appetite. One ought to be doing something at any point in time – a sluggard does nothing productive.

Best thing is a very developed appetite, which is never fulfilled.

A sluggard of a woman does not know God. God's oversight of everything He has created means He does not sleep or slumber.

Proverbs 14:23 says *All hard work brings a profit, but mere talk leads only to poverty.*

All hard work brings a profit. Everything you get after hard work is your profit – it cannot be anything else. God's principles for life are enduring – you work you get.

In **Proverbs 3; 16** Solomon says *Long life is in her right hand; in her left hand are riches and honour.*

It may not be in the number of years as humans know it – but her legacy will sustain her posterity.

This woman teaches her children so well so that after her, her children will live right.

This woman has benefit in both worlds – her right and her left.

Her riches came from her hard work, and man will honour her.

Such a woman God will also honour – she does not have time for gossip or for small talk, she thinks big, buying land and fields whilst others are thinking about teaspoons and forks.

This woman will love God because she sees the significance of God in her works.

She lives by the statement of Proverbs 24;3 *By wisdom a house is built, and through understanding it is established;*

She also remembers **Proverbs 14;15** The *simple believe anything, but the prudent give thought to their steps.*

A wise woman gives thought to her steps – the lives of her children and the welfare of her husband depend on it.

This woman is a super vessel.

She thinks, she is logical, she is smart.

Amongst Solomon's many proverbs is **Proverbs 12;24** *Diligent hands will rule, but laziness ends in forced labour.*

This is as good as it gets.

Town and country, home and away, we all want to rule.

Solomon is just saying work hard woman.

Stop complaining about your husband's authority.

She Is Clothed With Strength And Dignity and Laughs Without Fear Of The Future

You have yours – your authority comes from your hard work.

You psyche yourself, you talk to you. You self-command, you dare to dream, you are your own coordinator, cheerleader and enabler – only if you spend time – alone – with God.

In **2 Kings 8**, we read the story of Elisha and a certain woman.

The Bible says

Then spake Elisha unto the woman, whose son he had restored to life, saying, Arise, and go thou and thine household, and sojourn wheresoever thou canst sojourn: for the LORD hath called for a famine; and it shall also come upon the land seven years.

² And the woman arose, and did after the saying of the man of God: and she went with her household, and sojourned in the land of the Philistines seven years.

³ And it came to pass at the seven years' end, that the woman returned out of the land of the Philistines: and she went forth to cry unto the king for her house and for her land.

⁴ And the king talked with Gehazi the servant of the man of God, saying, Tell me, I pray thee, all the great things that Elisha hath done.

5 And it came to pass, as he was telling the king how he had restored a dead body to life, that, behold, the woman, whose son he had restored to life, cried to the king for her house and for her land. And Gehazi said, My Lord, O king, this is the woman, and this is her son, whom Elisha restored to life.

6 And when the king asked the woman, she told him. So the king appointed unto her a certain officer, saying, Restore all that was hers, and all the fruits of the field since the day that she left the land, even until now.

As women, we have nothing to fear, except we forget:

- Famine was there, and God had said it was going to be there, even when the woman had a house and her land.
- The same God who allowed the seven-year famine will create coincidences that will allow you to get back your house and your land. The Lord restores.
- Women can worship God with their substance. The women of Luke 8 had substance. They may probably not have ministered with Paul if they were going to be asking their husbands about every little thing.

Human beings get irritable when the asking is incessant.

Incessant is non-stop, never ending, ceaseless, continuous and continual, unremitting and relentless.

Too much asking is like a drizzle that never stops.

That level of asking creates cold weather; it creates muddy roads that are hard to walk on.

Luke reports in chapter 8

And it came to pass afterward, that he went throughout every city and village, preaching and shewing the glad tidings of the kingdom of God: and the twelve were with him,

2 And certain women, which had been healed of evil spirits and infirmities, Mary called Magdalene, out of whom went seven devils,

3 And Joanna the wife of Chuza Herod's steward, and Susanna, and many others, which ministered unto him of their substance **[Luke 8:1-3].**

Girded with strength and dignity, we stay positive

Culture can make women men dependant, but God liberates them.

To what extent is how far you spend time with your God – for God will take you through the famine in a foreign land, and will direct exactly when you shall see the king – so that you get your house and your land back.

He who makes everything beautiful in His time, when He goes before us, will make all the crooked places straight.

Seven years in the land of the Philistines, a foreign land, especially for the child of God, can be overwhelming, but when the Lord speaks, we know we will recover.

Good harvest will come, the famine will end – somehow sometime.

Hannah, in 1st Samuel, praying, says for by strength shall no man prevail.

As we go about our business, buying and planting, we cannot forget, for by strength shall no man prevail.

STEP 9

REJECTS MEDIOCRITY

A hard working, industrious, meticulous, thorough and attentive woman rejects the ordinary.

She cares about what she buys or sells – her merchandise.

She is diligent.

She frequently asks herself – "what quality" am I dealing with and in?

This woman strives for excellence.

Solomon says that woman *perceiveth that her merchandise is good: her candle goeth not out by night* **[Proverbs 31:18].**

Rejection of mediocrity is a message that is passed on quietly, subtly, without being contemptuous.

The Bible mentions Lydia and the quality of her merchandise. – Purple.

Acts 16:14-20 says

And a certain woman named Lydia, a seller of purple, of the city of Thyatira, which worshipped God, heard us: whose heart the Lord opened, that she attended unto the things which were spoken of Paul.

15 And when she was baptized, and her household, she besought us, saying, If ye have judged me to be faithful to the Lord, come into my house, and abide there. And she constrained us.

In everyday life and during the life of the Acts of the Apostles, purple means and meant priesthood, kingship, royalty, mediator and wealth, according to

https://www.colour-meanings.com/purple-colour-meaning-the-colour-purple/ and other researchers.

Quoting directly from same source, purple combines the **stability** of the blue colour and the **energy** of the red.

The lady Lydia could have chosen any other colour to deal with – white, for example. But she was a discerning lady – she knew what was significant, what made a difference.

The woman Lydia had a message to send – that she was trading stability and energy.

There is nothing better to define a woman of substance – it is not outside beauty, it is a stable personality.

A woman of substance is grounded in Godly principles.

She Is Clothed With Strength And Dignity and Laughs Without Fear Of The Future

In God Alone

She is simple, yet not simplistic.

Stability is all of the following – constancy, steadiness, firmness, solidity, permanence, immovability and strength.

A woman who spends time with God is not wishy washy, changing direction as soon as the wind direction changes.

She is consistent and has constancy. She establishes what she wants and pursues her vision.

She knows what she wants for her household and is not unnecessarily influenced to change course every waking moment.

She works to complete what (the good works) she started.

There is no blinking, there is focus.

This woman is steady. She does not panic.

Life will happen as it does – daily, in season and out of season. The steady woman will stop to think before she acts.

She asks herself all the essential questions, answering to and for herself in objective fashion, consistent with her faith and her beliefs.

She Is Clothed With Strength And Dignity and Laughs Without Fear Of The Future

This is the woman lady Lydia ministers to with her colour purple.

This woman is firm. She has principles that she lives by.

She does not let her emotions speak for her. She has her foundations firm on her God – He who lives from everlasting to everlasting.

She is not just firm, she is solid, resolute, unwavering, determined.

There is a sense of permanence in what she does. She puts effort in her work, because she is not a temporary person.

She approaches life issues with a sense of belonging – to a group of God-fearing people, to a tribe into which she is married, to her place of employment – at home or elsewhere.

She is a high value person – values everything and everyone.

When she sets her mind to work – she works. She is immovable. Knows what she stands for.

She is Godly.

She is endowed with strength and dignity.

This woman is the woman Solomon yearned to find.

She Is Clothed With Strength And Dignity and Laughs Without Fear Of The Future

In God Alone

It is not surprising that Solomon had a hard time finding one. His women worshipped other gods – who neither saw nor heard.

Our God is the Creator of the Universe, the Giver of Life, whose word is quick and powerful, sharper than any two-edged sword.

This is the God who guards and guides this woman.

This God, is her Lord Protector.

This woman, exudes energy and stability. She is the definition of the colour purple!

She has energy. This means she has all of the following: vigour, liveliness, get up and go, oomph, dynamism, vitality, drive and verve.

She is made to succeed.

Solomon was probably thinking about these qualities when he said *She perceiveth that her merchandise is good: her candle goeth not out by night.*

A woman who is full of energy has vigour.

When she walks everyone can tell she is walking. She does not run, lest she falls, she is not too hasty, she does not crawl because crawling is for babies and the infirm – she walks.

A good walk is not in your swing, it is in directness of the walk, the conviction that where you are going is good for you and all.

A good walk is purposeful.

She is lively.

She receives people with an out stretched hand. She does not act confused or flirty, but lively.

Those she interacts with love her demeanour. She is welcoming and convincing.

Her confidence speaks of her inner buoyancy – cheerfulness, enthusiasm, optimism – everything that a God-fearing woman ought to be.

She is a get up and go lady – she does not sleep on the job. She does not wait for instructions. She knows each season by name.

This woman knows how to read the time.

She is sure. She can plan – acknowledging God in all her ways.

She can execute, for God gives her strength. When she has done what she does – the work speaks for her.

She is dynamic.

She Is Clothed With Strength And Dignity and Laughs Without Fear Of The Future

When she speaks she is believed and believable. She lives the life she talks about. She is not fake or pretentious. She is the real deal. What you see is what you get.

This woman does not waste her energy – she is positively driven. Her energy goes for best reward. She does not sit and look when there is work to do or a contribution to be made.

This woman is a driver – of herself and of her situation or circumstance. She is not problem or challenge focused, she is solution driven.

This is the woman lady Lydia was "selling".

The one who sells purple knows there are imitators, those that sell violet!

The difference between violet and purple is that violet is displayed in the visible light spectrum, while purple is simply a mixture of red and blue.

Colourmeanings.com. Purple Colour Meaning. [online]

This is what separates humankind - imitators.

It is noted that although violet is not quite as intense as purple, their essence is the same. The imitators just don't execute, they talk.

The imitators want to hide. They are *the also ran*.

The imitators you need to get a binocular to see exactly who they are. The genuine are easily identifiable, they have nothing to hide.

The woman who spends time with the Maker will be able to distinguish the difference between violet and purple – the close resemblers against the real.

The narrative says that generally speaking, the names are interchangeable and the meaning of the colours is the same.

Wow!

The names may be interchangeable, but a woman who spends time with God will not be mistaken. Her actions cannot be interchanged with another's. She is distinct, she is not grey.

This woman is stable and energetic – she is spiritual and physical.

Her stability expands her horizon and connects her to a higher level of consciousness.

The woman wears stability like a well-fitting and appropriate dress. She is not myopic. She is well observing. She is knowledgeable and full of wisdom. She understands her calling.

She knows she will walk this earth for a season and soon she is gone – as David says – like a flower. She does not waste time with the here and now – she thinks about the future.

She has a higher level of consciousness – she has a spirit that correctly discerns issues. She knows what she ought to do and does it – in time and space.

Stability demands that you be practical.

There is harmony of emotions and the mind. A stable woman is peaceful, synchronising in perfect harmony thought and action.

She knows she cannot speak all she thinks and she thinks before she speaks.

This woman Solomon is envisaging is selfless. She feels.

The "colour" of a woman means she is sensitive to all the different types of pollution in the world today, whether it is air pollution, noise pollution, visual pollution or contamination.

This sensitivity makes a woman susceptible to diseases and allergies, and vulnerable to her own familiar surroundings.

This woman knows her situation.

She takes time to understand the pollution that is in the world today.

She guards (by prayer) her family against all levels and types of pollution.

The woman is selective of what she feeds on, what she hears and what she sees.

She is a no-nonsense woman. She rejects mediocrity.

This woman knows that what affects a woman most is not what is distant, but whatever is immediate and familiar.

This woman is uniquely placed to handle issues as they come. She does not tire or give up, but she knows to cover herself and her own against potential hazards of disease, allergies and other vulnerabilities of contamination.

She understands the hazards of dangerous liaisons.

The "purple woman" Lydia is selling is creative and inspired.

She is original. She does not do because another did. She recreates for her own good and comfort of her household.

This woman is not one of a crowd.

She leaves people wondering how she does it – but she does. She is positively independent.

This woman has power but very humble – brain power mixed with her humility makes her stand out.

She is so stable she knows when and how power should and can be exercised.

Her bottom line is – she cannot accept mediocrity, for herself and for others. She has a powerful understanding of where her help comes from.

Her help comes from the Lord, who made heaven and earth.

This kind of woman will not accept anything for free. She knows value is always in exchange.

The narration from Genesis about Abraham buying a field is loaded with meaning. It reflects one who cares about what she (in this case) sells or buys - her merchandise.

Good merchandise comes from refined personalities; decency, modesty, dignity, correctness, courtesy, discretion and politeness in everyday living.

Bible narrative says Abraham bought an expensive field to bury his wife. He was given a field but he chose to pay for it – fair value. Abraham paid *current money with the merchant (verse 16).*

From **Genesis 23:11** the narration reads

Nay, my Lord, hear me: the field give I thee, and the cave that is therein, I give it thee; in the presence of the sons of my people give I it thee: bury thy dead.

12 And Abraham bowed down himself before the people of the land.

13 And he spake unto Ephron in the audience of the people of the land, saying, But if thou wilt give it, I pray thee, hear me: I will give thee money for the field; take it of me, and I will bury my dead there.

14 And Ephron answered Abraham, saying unto him,

15 My Lord, hearken unto me: the land is worth four hundred shekels of silver; what is that betwixt me and thee? bury therefore thy dead.

16 And Abraham hearkened unto Ephron; and Abraham weighed to Ephron the silver, which he had named in the audience of the sons of Heth, four hundred shekels of silver, current money with the merchant.

17 And the field of Ephron which was in Machpelah, which was before Mamre, the field, and the cave which was therein, and all the trees that were in the field, that were in all the borders round about, were made sure

18 Unto Abraham for a possession in the presence of the children of Heth, before all that went in at the gate of his city.

She Is Clothed With Strength And Dignity and Laughs Without Fear Of The Future

¹⁹ *And after this, Abraham buried Sarah his wife in the cave of the field of Machpelah before Mamre:*

Abraham made sure the field, and the cave, and the trees that were in the field, were legally his – he rejected assumption, he preferred certainty.

Reject mediocrity, even to bury your dead.

In a foreign land, the natives knew the person they were dealing with was a prince and they say to Abraham *thou art a mighty prince among us: in the choice of our sepulchres bury thy dead.*

Abraham quickly mentions the place he wants Sarah buried. He did not mumble, he did not ask to get it for free – it was fair market value.

Free gifts are costlier than paid for – pay for what you get.

Price, is an assumption of value.

The field that Abraham bought was so good generations were buried on it, and the new testament of the Bible refers to it.

Quality lasts, mediocrity is cheap.

A woman, who spends time alone, with God, can do the mathematics!

She Is Clothed With Strength And Dignity and Laughs Without Fear Of The Future

STEP 10

IN CONTROL

My definition of control is, the ability to regulate, to set the rules, to govern.

Control is not an end in itself, it is an attitude, and it is an ethic.

Control effort is governed by the moral principles that govern one's behaviour or activity, by one's way of thinking or feeling about something.

It is an approach, an outlook, on life and everything that it brings.

Solomon creates a view of a woman that is totally in control of her faculties. The woman is so mature and aligned with what is at stake.

Solomon says *She layeth her hands to the spindle, and her hands hold the distaff* **[Proverbs 31:19]**

This is huge.

The woman has and is in control. Her hands are full – her hands hold the spindle and her hands hold the distaff.

She Is Clothed With Strength And Dignity and Laughs Without Fear Of The Future

When she decides to do anything – she assumes ownership.

There are various spindles defined, ranging from machines to body cell structures.

The spindle Solomon is referring to is arguably the one defined as a straight spike usually made from wood used for spinning, twisting fibres such as wool, flax, hemp and cotton, into yarn.

Researchers say before the invention of the spinning wheel; the spinning of yarn or thread was traditionally done by women using a spindle and a distaff. A spindle was a long spool to hold and spin the yarn. A distaff was a short rod with an opening or branches at the top for holding the flax or wool.

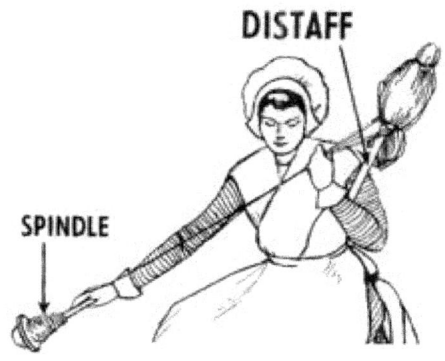

https://en.wikipedia.org/wiki/Distaf

The woman who held the distaff had to be strong physically and mentally. Spinning was the most likely trade of women in Solomon's time.

In this day and age, what women can do, was beyond Solomon's imagination.

When Jesus walked this earth a lot more women enterprises were evident.

One such was tent making. Acts 18 gives a short narrative of one who was in tent making, partnering her husband in the business.

The Bible says,

18 After these things Paul departed from Athens, and came to Corinth;

2 And found a certain Jew named Aquila, born in Pontus, lately come from Italy, with his wife Priscilla; (because that Claudius had commanded all Jews to depart from Rome:) and came unto them.

3 And because he was of the same craft, he abode with them, and wrought: for by their occupation they were tentmakers.

Husband and wife worked together.

The Bible found it necessary to add what they did for their livelihood. Our occupation is important to God.

Tent making is not an easy occupation. It demands hard work, as much as spinning the yarn. It's an occupation that has spanned the whole of human existence, from Abraham to Paul to this day. It is therefore worth referencing.

Tents are mentioned in the Bible; for example, in **Genesis 4:20** Jabal is described as *'the first to live in tents and raise sheep and goats'*.

Tents are largely meant to provide portable shelter for any number of people in the field, and to shelter support activities and supplies.

Everyone who chooses an occupation or profession wants to provide a service.

The product ought to meet certain standards and criteria.

This means Aquila and Priscilla were selling tents for what tents can do and provide.

Tents accommodate. A tent maker seeks to accommodate.

Tents protect against inclement weather.

The tent maker's message is – prepare – the weather may turn bad.

What they use and how they construct the tent becomes important and very relevant.

To highlight the issues, some sections of the narration below are direct quotations, whilst the bulleted points are the learning points in this analogy, on tenant making.

https://www.wikihow.com/Make-a-Tent and
https://en.wikipedia.org/wiki/Tent,

"The first part of tenant making is tying a frame.

- A frame shapes what you want to create. Our frame of mind as people, and especially for women, is the beginning of what can be.
- In life, a woman who spends time with God is well framed. Her vision, her purpose is shaped by what role she wants to play in the destiny of her household, community and the world.
- She is cognisant of the materials she has and what she will need. Building a quick and easy makeshift tent doesn't require a lot. Building a tent that lasts does.

A good tent cannot be built on rugged terrain. There is risk of piercing the material. The builder needs to locate a good support system for the frame.

A tent will need trees or poles close enough to tie your rope but far enough to fit your covers.

In God Alone

- All firm foundations are set on something firmer than what one wants to build.
- We can only anchor on powers bigger and stronger than ourselves.
- We need a more enduring spirit – the poles of our lives.
- The poles we use cannot be people, because people err and fall, they are not consistent, they change.

The tent ought to be built on good height and elevation. Too high becomes extremely cold during the evening.

- When one speaks of elevation and height – one is just looking beyond the familiar. When one is sitting or standing, or whatever posture they are in, it is from that posture that they can only look up or elevate – for better vision. You cannot remain the same when you elevate yourself or gain a height advantage. This does not matter where you are or where you were born. It's a principle of life. Elevate yourself and gain some height advantage – issues of life become clearer.

It is a concept of human existence that valleys will collect water in rainy seasons.

- Rains differ, but whether it's a short heavy down pour or an incessant drizzle, the effect is

She Is Clothed With Strength And Dignity and Laughs Without Fear Of The Future

the same. You cannot pitch your tent in the valley.

Tents should not be pitched beneath dead branches – these branches fall when the storm comes.

- Many times, women are caught up in situations where humanity concludes women do not think. This is not correct. At times, however, women do not think through. Thinking through means you can see the dead branches under your tree. Some women get comfortable in very perilous situations and circumstances. They need to set their hands on the spindle and hold their distaff.

Damp ground makes for easy adherence of canvas to ground, prevents dust around the tent.

- There are instances where one needs to make damp the ground. A stiff neck will not get anyone anywhere. Where one needs to compromise in a positive way, then let it be. The important thing is to know how and when. You cannot compromise whilst under a dead branch of some tree.

The tent rope tied to trees or trunks needs to be heavy duty. The rope is wrapped around the trees a few times before the knot is tied. Anything heavy duty is stable and lasts better than its light weight alternative.

In God Alone

- Heavy duty does not get easily blown by the wind. It has capacity to stand. Women that spend time alone with God can stand most of what is thrown at them when life happens.

Where and how the heavy-duty rope is tied to the tree or pole determines how comfortable staying in the tent will be. Too low makes the going in and out and living in the tent challenging.

- Low living is not, and can never be part of Godly lifestyle. Prudent women tie their ropes, doubling down on the precepts and promises of their God. Not once, not even twice, so many times such that no wind or tide can move them.

Where the rope is tied too high, the canvass will not be able to reach the ground. For those that pitch tents, the narration is: err on the side of caution and tie your rope a good amount lower than half of the length of your canvas.

- A woman that understands that life does happen, will take care not to live above their means. The canvas still needs to touch the ground. These women are not proud, they are humble.
- These women know that when what they have is folded, they still need to be covered and comfortable. Prudent women know that their

canvass ought to fold well. A tent is not complete if it remains open. When the tent is folded, its occupants should still be covered and comfortable.

The ground where you lay your tent ought to be free of rocks, pebbles, twigs and anything that might poke holes in it.

- The tent maker cannot take anything for granted. Life is not a given. There are no guarantees.
- What a woman who spends time with God does is to prepare. Remove the rocks and the twigs – the complaining, the murmuring, the bitterness, the anger, the sulking, the ungratefulness, and the and the and the. Those things will only poke holes in your tent and make your life in your tent uncomfortable.
- A woman that spends time with God checks where she sits, where she stands and where she walks.

  You cannot afford to sit, stand and or walk anyhow – there are things that a prudent woman can simply not do, places where she simply can't go, things she simply can't say, and imaginations that she simply can't entertain.

In God Alone

A comfortable canvass floor should not have wrinkles. It should be smoothed out.

- It takes effort to smooth out wrinkles. When one talks wrinkles it seems a small thing – its huge. A woman ought to put her best face forward. That means smoothing out the wrinkles in your life. This, at times, means prayer and supplication. There is nothing too small to fast for – if whatever it is, makes your life unproductive and challenging.

As the placing of the ground canvass is important, determining where occupant will be *vis a vis* the heavy-duty rope; the canvas should be placed in such a way that it is centred between the trees and directly beneath the rope.

- The rope and the trees determine how the canvas will be fixed, its strength and how it looks. A woman that spends time with God knows exactly where she ought to stay, centred between the Lord God and His Christ, under the tutoring of the Holy Spirit.

Securing the canvas is not a small thing. Some canvasses have holes on their corners that are ready made where poles are thrust through and hammered to the ground for security.

- A woman's cover needs to be hammered to the ground. Hammers and hard rocks will do the job. A woman's canvas is her faith. Sometimes it takes hammers and rocks to ground your faith.

The hammering is done twice; the second time is when the walls are being built. First time hammering is meant to fix the ground canvass but is not too deep; it has to be firmed up after the walls are raised.

- As the family grows, relationships grow. The walls are put up and the walls – those relationships, cannot stand unless your faith is hammered to the ground. Nothing is cheap in tent making. Even pushing through steel stakes in ready-made tent holes requires effort.

Adjust when you see that your canvass walls are not touching the ground.

- When canvas walls are not touching the ground, there is bound to be trouble. Your faith ought to touch the ground. It's your belief system, it's your mind set, it is who you are.

The canvass walls also need to be secured to the ground.

The ground canvass and the walls need to be tied and secured by the same stakes or rocks.

- You cannot afford to separate where you sit and live – the ground – with your walls – your faith. When the two are separated, there is disharmony and life in the tent will show that the connections are not right. God gives insight – to see where the connections are and whether or not they need addressing, and exactly how to fix them That requires plenty of wisdom. Only God can give that wisdom.

Make sure your tent is protected around to avoid running water flowing into your tent – build mounds or dig a trench.

- What you use to protect you and your tent from running water depends on where you are. If on a slope, trenches will do, if on level ground, then mounds will do. Do what it takes to survive – in a Godly way. Rains will come. A prudent woman will prepare for the eventuality.

There will always be common problems to trouble shoot.

- Life will happen. Everyday has its challenges. Trouble shooting is an art. You cannot shoot anywhere and anyhow. There is a correct set of tools for every problem. Wrong application of the right tools will definitely mean disaster. Correctness is in time and place. The what, many will know. Knowledge, understanding and wisdom will determine the variables – of time and place. Anything done out of time and place is not correct.

If you do not have steel stakes to pin down your tent, use tree branches – just whittle one end until there is a point.

- Be flexible, look around and see what you have and use it. A significant number of women will take changeable situations and circumstances as unchangeable because they are not flexible. Anything that cannot bend of its own accord will break when forced to.

    Nature tells of the palm tree – the righteous shall flourish like the palm tree – so says David.

    It is not because the palm tree does not meet challenges, it adapts and strengthens itself.

    The palm tree will bend and allow the storm to pass over. It will surely rise again when the weather is more amenable.

When the steel stakes or pegs are not there, use tree branches – that is what you have.

- You cannot stand in the rain because the steel pegs are not there. Look around, tree branches are everywhere.

Tree branches for stakes ought to be thin enough to fit in the holes but thick enough to not break.

- If you can snap it easily with your hands it's probably not strong enough. Tree branches come in all shapes and sizes. Take the ones that fit into your tent holes. You cannot copy what Mrs Sugar is doing when you are Mrs Salt. Your lives are as different as your finger prints. Perhaps, you are just at the opposite ends of the spectrum, but if you both know God, the rope that ties you will be the same, all heavy duty and enduring.

There are times when one can make a tent with only one tree.

- If you can't find two trees that are a good distance apart, you can make a tent of a different shape with one tree. The method, the framing, the roping, the everything, will be different.

The shapes of the tents will necessarily be different.

All depends on the weather, the number of occupants, intended use and duration of use. Many factors affect tent design, but most important are two factors – financial cost and intended use.

Financial cost - The least expensive tents tend to be heavier, less durable and less waterproof. The most expensive tents, used by serious backpackers and professional adventurers, are usually lighter in weight, more durable and more waterproof.

Intended use – Tents meant for backpacking implies lengthy duration for carrying the tent; weight and size become the most crucial factors. Tents used in touring imply high frequency of pitching and striking the tent. For that purpose, ease of pitching/striking the tent becomes important. A static situation means staying at one campsite for a week or two at a time.

- A comfortable camping experience is the target.

A summary of tents and tent making, as quoted from acknowledged websites, indicates that;

A tent is a shelter consisting of sheets of fabric or other material draped over, attached to a frame of poles or attached to a supporting rope. While smaller tents may be free-standing or attached to the ground, large tents are usually anchored using guy ropes tied to stakes or tent pegs.

- This means that the material used to create and set up a tent is critical.

A simple tented shelter can be made of any material such as cotton (canvas), nylon, felt and polyester.

Cotton absorbs water, so it can become heavy when wet, but the associated swelling tends to block any minute holes so that wet cotton is more waterproof than dry cotton.

Nylon and polyester are much lighter than cotton and do not absorb much water; with suitable coatings they can be very waterproof, but they tend to deteriorate over time due to a slow chemical breakdown caused by ultraviolet light.

- The size of the tent and its location determines how it will be built.

Tents are built for purpose – ranging from tents big enough for one person to sleep in, up to huge circus tents capable of seating thousands of people.

In summary;

Women who spend time with God know, that all tenant factors determine the time it would take to pitch and dismantle the tent.

They know what matters in life, for them and for others.

These women provide, as much as they build tenants, quick and easy solutions to challenging situations.

They provide economical and practical solutions; solutions that save families, marriages, jobs, relationships, health.

They provide clean energy solutions to life.

These women do not call themselves "urban". They fit for the greater good.

They provide emergency shelter when called to do so. They are simply available, in the short term and even for the long haul.

These women are a blessing to the community. They are accessible.

These women can improvise.

These qualities separate tent makers.

Whilst the method of construction is basically the same, what separates good tents from the rest, or good tent makers from the rest, are the details and the resolve.

Further, the quoted article states that "there are three basic configurations of tents, each of which may appear with many variations:

1. Single skin: Only one waterproof layer of fabric is used, comprising at least roof and walls.
2. Single skin with flysheet: A waterproof flysheet or rain fly is suspended over and clear of the roof of the tent; it often overlaps the tent roof slightly, but does not extend down the sides or ends of the tent
3. Double skin (double wall): The outer tent is a waterproof layer which extends down to the ground all round. One or more 'inner tents' provide sleeping areas".

My thinking is, whether you use a single skin, single skin with flysheet or you double wall your tent, depends on how you assess the weather – your situation and your circumstance.

Another article states,

https://en.wikipedia.org/wiki/Tent

"A tent required only for summer use may be very different from one to be used in the depths of winter. Manufacturers label tents as one-season, two/three-season, three/four season, four season, etc.

A one-season tent is generally for summer use only, and may only be capable of coping with light showers. A three-season tent is for spring/summer/autumn and should be capable of withstanding fairly heavy rain, or very light snow. A four-season tent should be suitable for winter camping in all but the most extreme conditions; an expedition tent (for mountain conditions) should be strong enough to cope with heavy snow, strong winds, as well as heavy rain.

Some tents are sold, quite cheaply, as festival tents; these may be suitable only for camping in dry weather, and may not even be showerproof".

My conclusion is:

Women and their lives, is the story of tent making.

How you make your tent depends on you.

Woman, take control of your camping season.

STEP 11

SAINTLY

Saints are the redeemed of the Lord.

Whilst we wait for our Saviour Jesus Christ to take us home, we who love the Lord have a duty to do – towards the infirm and the needy in our families and the community.

Our way of doing things should cover those that cannot. Solomon realised this need and figured when a woman is endowed with Godly character she can make a difference.

Sometimes the demands are so overwhelming we are tempted to complain and give up, but a woman who spends time alone with God will stay the course – she will remain faithful even when her heart is overwhelmed.

This woman prays for everyday wisdom. She is a difference maker, every time everywhere.

Solomon says this woman, in **Proverbs 31:20** *stretcheth out her hand to the poor; yea, she reacheth forth her hands to the needy*

She Is Clothed With Strength And Dignity and Laughs Without Fear Of The Future

A typical Bible character with this virtue is described in **Acts 9:36-42**.

The narrative says

[36] *Now there was at Joppa a certain disciple named Tabitha, which by interpretation is called Dorcas: this woman was full of good works and alms deeds which she did.*

[37] *And it came to pass in those days, that she was sick, and died: whom when they had washed, they laid her in an upper chamber.*

[38] *And forasmuch as Lydda was nigh to Joppa, and the disciples had heard that Peter was there, they sent unto him two men, desiring him that he would not delay to come to them.*

[39] *Then Peter arose and went with them. When he was come, they brought him into the upper chamber: and all the widows stood by him weeping, and shewing the coats and garments which Dorcas made, while she was with them.*

[40] *But Peter put them all forth, and kneeled down, and prayed; and turning him to the body said, Tabitha, arise. And she opened her eyes: and when she saw Peter, she sat up.*

[41] *And he gave her his hand, and lifted her up, and when he had called the saints and widows, presented her alive.*

[42] *And it was known throughout all Joppa; and many believed in the Lord.*

She Is Clothed With Strength And Dignity and Laughs Without Fear Of The Future

In God Alone

It is not in vain that we follow Christ.

Dorcas was a disciple of Christ.

This means she followed Christ. A follower believes and acts like the leader. Dorcas remembered Jesus cared.

She did not just do the good works – she could because she was full of them. It was in her, it was her character.

Dorcas cared. Caring is saintly.

Saintly is being good and Godly, it is being pious and virtuous.

Saintly is being devout, righteous and holy.

In Dorcas was all these and more.

The Dorcas report shows even disciples full of good works die – it's not always easy or smooth. Hard times will come. When hard times come, the good works will "speak" for you.

For me, this means that it is not in vain that we follow Christ.

When a woman spends time with God – it is for inspiration, for strength, for Godly insight, for wisdom and for life.

She Is Clothed With Strength And Dignity and Laughs Without Fear Of The Future

History records a story of a woman who was born in an esteemed family but chose to work in one of the subservient jobs available – at that time. This is the story of Florence Nightingale:

The Nurse https://britishheritage.com/florence-nightingale/

The story of Florence starts by her noticing or seeing something was wrong. The narration says

"She began to notice that many of the popular treatments available—bloodletting, administering infusions of arsenic, mercury, and opiates—were actually killing more patients than they saved. She believed and began proving she could save more patients from death by caring for their basic needs— keeping them warm, clean, rested, and well-fed."

It's the basics that often make the difference in life – not the huge high maintenance house, not the huge luxury Bentleys of our time, not Air Force 1 jet life – the basics – keeping warm, clean, rested and well fed.

The summary of Florence's life indicates she chose a point of impact and it presented itself in the Crimean war in 1854.

Quoted research says "Florence worked to improve conditions in the hospitals. She and her nurses bathed the soldiers, washed their linens, and fed them more substantial food. She eventually established a separate kitchen with her own money to prepare easily digested food for patients. She secured a source of clean drinking water and improved overall sanitary conditions. She set up a system for receiving patients, the basis of modern triage. The mortality rate declined 2% because of her efforts. She personally attended to countless men, many on their deathbeds. She made so many endless rounds, carrying a lamp with her in the late hours of the night, that she became known as the "Lady with the Lamp," a nickname that was published in an account of her work in The London Times."

- It takes spiritual eyes to see and to do, for that is what the Bible says – the Lord gives us the power to will and to do. The tragedy is those who have say the needy are too needy, and those who do not have say we cannot, folding their hands in resignation.
- What we need to do is listen to what God says. The instructions are clear, and the Lord will direct our paths.

History records that "Florence Nightingale was born on 12 May 1820 into a rich, upper-class, well-connected British family at the *Villa Colombaia*".

These three lines summarise a life of privilege.

Florence did not have a reason to go into a war zone, but she did.

In God Alone

She listened to her conscience and sub conscience. She listened to the voice of an invisible God, an invincible God.

It is recorded that "Nightingale believed God called her to service in February 1837".

Florence put a signature to her work. This is who she was:

Born 12 May 1820. Florence, Grand Duchy of Tuscany

Died 13 August 1910 (aged 90). Mayfair, London, England

Nationality British

Known for Pioneering modern nursing

Awards Royal Red Cross (1883)
Lady of Grace of the Order of St John (LGStJ) (1904)
Order of Merit (1907)

Scientific career

Fields Hospital hygiene and sanitation, statistics

Institutions Selimiye Barracks, Scutari. King's College London[1]

Signature *Florence Nightingale*

She Is Clothed With Strength And Dignity and Laughs Without Fear Of The Future

The year 1837 is almost 200 years ago, yet Florence's hospital rules are the basis of care even in this 21st century.

As I read more about the lady Florence Nightingale, I was inspired to work more, do more, regardless of a seemingly privileged life.

Seemingly because it is a grace filled life. I, have received grace, a lot of grace.

That grace, should push anyone to do exceptional things. Things that last, things that defy time, things that change lives, for the here and now, and also for eternity.

That grace, is from God. The grace to power-shovel for God.

What Florence did was not for the money. She did what she did from the heart.

She was a "bright, tough, driven professional, a brilliant organizer and statistician, and one of the most influential women in 19th-century England."

Given these inspiring characters like Dorcas of the Bible and Florence Nightingale of almost 200 years ago, I hope to put my signature, to the works that grace will have me do.

In God Alone

One article says "Florence Nightingale was distinctly not the romantic, retiring Victorian gentlewoman most of us imagine".

Attending to the poor and needy does not mean mediocrity.

Attending to the poor and needy means moving around with your lamp in front of you, chest out, and head up.

It means doing all for the glory of God.

The work ethic that Florence had, is the same that is demanded today – brilliant ideas and fool proof planning, tough mentality, driving professionalism, hard core organisation and clean accounting.

The article of reference notes;

She Is Clothed With Strength And Dignity and Laughs Without Fear Of The Future

"She is a "ministering angel" without any exaggeration in these hospitals, and as her slender form glides quietly along each corridor, every poor fellow's face softens with gratitude at the sight of her. When all the medical officers have retired for the night and silence and darkness have settled down upon those miles of prostrate sick, she may be observed alone, with a little lamp in her hand, making her solitary rounds".

https://en.wikipedia.org/wiki/Florence_Nightingale

As children of God, our lamp will not fail; we cannot run out of fuel or flickers.

We cannot be exhausted, for we are sustained by the grace of our God.

The word of God is our lamp. It is the difference maker.

Dorcas did not have much, she did not sell purple, but she used what she had. Florence had all, and she used that which she had to bring a smile to someone's face.

Saintly women spend time alone with God.

These women enquire from God, even as they seek the face of God.

The world, as we know it, is a great wilderness. Goodness is in short supply.

Saintly women will make a difference.

Saintly women will heal the world, not because they have high IQs, but because they "walk with God".

This is all the world needs – healing.

The world needs healing in all its shapes and sizes; physical healing and spiritual healing.

The world needs social healing, emotional healing and mental healing.

Dorcas, Florence, and You, are the ladies who did, the ladies who do and the ladies who define and separate the good from the bad.

They did and they do, not by power or by might, but because grace found them.

A woman that spends time with God makes the difference – they are not saints – they are simply saintly.

STEP 12

ABUNDANT FAITH

At some stage in our lives, some moment in time, we have all feared something.

Nicodemus and Joseph of Arimathea feared the institutions they belonged to.

Some children fear darkness, some husbands fear their wives and some wives fear their husbands.

Employees fear their employers.

Fear is the art of life – for flight or fight. Fear often shapes our decisions, rightly or wrongly.

We fear because we are not all there. At times we want something different from what we can get or can have.

However, fear replaces faith.

Children of God, when they remember what the Lord said in His word, they know we, as children of God, were never given a spirit of fear, but of power, of love and a sound mind.

Those three attributes give us faith.

Proverbs 31:21 says a virtuous woman *is not afraid of the snow for her household: for all her household are clothed with scarlet.*

To not be afraid is huge. It signifies a sense of preparedness, a willingness to trust the eternal God.

Snow, for those that are exposed to it in one way or the other, is not something one can sit on or walk on barefooted. It can freeze everything in a few moments of time.

Whilst it may be beautiful to see snow topped mountains and snow filled valleys, that is all, as human beings, that we can contain.

When snow meets our warm bodies we all fold up.

The woman Solomon sees and imagines is one who does not fold up – she is prepared for the snow. The book of Hebrews in chapter 11 says

Now faith is the substance of things hoped for, the evidence of things not seen.

⁶ *But without faith it is impossible to please him: for he that cometh to God must believe that he is, and that he is a rewarder of them that diligently seek him.*

These are attributes of abundant faith, such attributes are not gender sensitive.

Faith is faith.

Faith does not make it easy, whatever it is, it just makes things possible.

The things we want, the things we need, the things we expect from our God, come into the line of possibilities.

Hebrews, as I have read it, is a book of faith.

It is also a book of reports. Paul to the Hebrews says this person did this and it was deemed faith.

The second verse of Hebrews 11 and the 39th verse talks about the same – obtaining a good report.

When faith is abundant we understand more of the things of God. We are not pressured by circumstances; we get good perspective on the issues of life.

Abel did and Cain did not. To these brothers, the teaching was the same, the background the same, the environment the same, but different was the output.

Their works, their thinking, produced different reports.

In the abundance of faith, we offer to God a more excellent sacrifice.

We do not take for granted the sacrifice of God for man.

In the abundance of faith, we value, cherish and protect the teachings of God.

Faith does not allow us to doubt.

With faith, we believe.

We believe that the Lord is a rewarder of those that diligently seek him.

God is faithful – when Enoch walked with Him, God translated him to heaven.

As we diligently seek God, in word and deed, we are simultaneously translated, from one level of faith to another. Our speech, our thoughts, our sight, our hearing, our work and our walk, all is changed, for God's glory.

In and by faith, we cannot remain the same. We cannot struggle to change character if we have faith in our God.

God perfects and transforms. What we do is believe, that He is able.

The invisible God, the invincible God. The God of all creation, also challenges our faith in Him.

Hebrews 7 says Noah moved with fear, prepared an ark for the saving of his house. This is Godly fear – positive fear. This is faith in context.

Faith in God pushes one to excellence in preparation, because the snow will come.

Preparation is instructive of faith. Instructions are performed by obedience.

The instructions come from the Lord.

The Lord says obeying is better than sacrifice, because obedience can never be defiled.

Obedience illustrates a higher mentality – the supremacy of God.

Faith then means when the Lord speaks through His word, man moves towards God and not away.

When we obey we can walk in the paths of this world with confidence, because we know He who promised is faithful.

We receive strength to receive the seed as Sarah deed; a seed to conceive.

Whatever we want and need ought to start somewhere. When the Lord is not in it, all becomes a waste of time and effort.

Obedience and faith are sisters. When we obey, we are then called faithful.

Faith actually clears our judgement. Faith removes shadows; faith makes heaven real, and life sublime.

Life becomes of elevated quality, even in the here and now.

In faith, life is beautiful, inspiring and uplifting.

Faith gives us courage to keep moving.

Faith persuades us to do all for Christ, to embrace who we are in Christ and to confess the magnificence of God in our lives.

Our speech will be a declaration of what we seek – a better place.

Our faith stops us from looking back at yesterday's ashes, we are propelled forward.

Faith gives greater vision – something better that does not pass away, something eternal.

Being faith grounded, the woman who spends time alone with God blesses others – children, grandchildren and all, she trusts posterity to do the right thing – carry her "bones" when the time is right.

Women that spend time with God, do not shy away from adversity, they face whatever comes with the confidence that says my "bones will survive" into the Promised Land!

Moses mother had that type of vision. She understood exactly where she was, what she needed to do and how.

She Is Clothed With Strength And Dignity and Laughs Without Fear Of The Future

The timing of all could only be done by those that spend time with God. It was not simple, it was intelligent.

When faith is abundant, titles cease to matter.

What becomes important is who knows your name.

Choices are clear – sin is not part of the equation of your life's transactions.

A woman who spends time with God knows an association with Christ is all there is – nothing less.

Faith forces one to forsake the mundane – Egypt, regardless of the consequences of leaving Egypt.

A faith based woman knows that worldly is ordinary.

A woman who spends time with God passes through where others fail.

The red sea of life needs God as the leader. To walk the paths and cross the rivers, to overcome the storms in the seas of this world, needs the faith of Jesus, faith in Jesus.

Faith focuses. The lady does not give up on what is good, till the walls (of their Jericho) fall.

Seven days and fourteen circles they will go, without complaint, without murmuring, without confusion, without losing steam, until the walls fall.

She Is Clothed With Strength And Dignity and Laughs Without Fear Of The Future

In God Alone

This woman knows she cannot perish like and with those that do not believe. The gulf is huge. The silence, the peace, the calm, is audible – those that spend time with God, in all their steps, are different.

This woman, faith filled, belongs to a generation of believers who subdue kingdoms and bring righteousness to families and communities.

She obtains promises as said by the Lord God Almighty is His word.

This woman stops the mouths of lions – not by confrontation, but in her gentleness and humility – she disempowers the unruly.

This woman is powerful. She is a great contender. She fights.

I love this woman. Her faith quenches the violence of fire, and escapes the edge of the sword.

This woman is made strong out of weakness, and she is waxed valiant in fight.

This lady turns to flight the armies of the aliens.

She is quiet in the outside, but a brazen wall inside.

She is a defended city.

She is not encumbered by the temporary; she can stand trial, and can overcome temptation.

She Is Clothed With Strength And Dignity and Laughs Without Fear Of The Future

In God Alone

This woman is not destitute in affliction, whether she wanders in deserts or mountains.

Although trials and temptations come, she does not lack in wisdom, knowledge and understanding.

She knows her faith will give her wings to fly, regardless of her circumstances.

She trusts her God, the Creator of the Universe.

By faith, this woman is focussed. She does not waver.

She has Godly principles, so her policies can never be wrong.

This woman operates above board; she stands on high moral ground.

This woman is exceptional, because what she knows to do, is lean on God.

What she knows to do, is learn from the Master, for the Master says,

Take my yoke upon you, and learn of me; for I am meek and lowly in heart: and ye shall find rest unto your souls **[Mathew 11:29].**

She does all, not by power, nor by might, but by the Spirit of the Lord.

This woman is faithful.

She Is Clothed With Strength And Dignity and Laughs Without Fear Of The Future

She is correct, she is true and realistic, she is authentic and exact.

This woman is truthful, to our God and to man.

Her faith overflows.

STEP 13

ELEGANT INDEPENDENCE

Caleb's daughter Achsah, married her cousin Othniel.

Othniel's father was called Kenaz, and was brother to Caleb, one of the two men that left Egypt and got to Canaan.

By any standard, theirs was a good marriage, a lot good "guaranteed".

Othniel had done well, he had conquered a city and his reward was Caleb's daughter.

A significant number of marriages are like Achsah's. All is well and there is nothing to worry about. Dad is there and the husband is a good man, but Solomon says, woman, weave your own coverings.

By inference, in **Proverbs 31:22**

Solomon says even "Achsah" *maketh herself coverings of tapestry; her clothing is silk and purple,*

As **Joshua 15:18** says

One day when she came to Othniel, she urged him to ask her father for a field. When she got off her donkey, Caleb asked her, "What can I do for you?"

¹⁹ She replied, "Do me a special favour. Since you have given me land in the Negev, give me also springs of water." So Caleb gave her the upper and lower springs.

Achsah was not satisfied with land in the Negev, without the springs of water.

She knew she would need the springs of water for her land to be productive.

Most women when married, have the land, but there are no springs of water in their lives.

We ought to go back to God, the giver of land and springs of water, and ask for our fair share.

It does not matter we are married to the good man of the land; we ought to be elegantly independent.

Elegance is not pride – it is a realisation that we are fearfully and wonderfully made. It is an acknowledgement of the grace God has bestowed upon us, as women.

That elegant independence does not come of itself; it requires that we give ourselves time to think.

Nothing will be dished out to women because they are women.

Solomon recognized and appreciated a woman that goes the mile to make herself comfortable – she makes for herself, herself.

What she makes is not ordinary – its coverings of tapestry. This takes time and effort.

Tapestry is defined as a heavy hand-woven, reversible textile used for hangings, curtains, and upholstery and characterized by complicated pictorial designs

It is not a statement of opulence, but of hard work, of a greater way of thinking, of putting form and image forward.

She has an established system, her own way of doing things.

She learns from others, but does not copy them, for she knows God did not create a blue print, each is her own person.

She has a practice, and she practises her handiwork.

One's handiwork defines what drives a person, their *raison d'être,* that is, the most important reason or purpose for someone or something's existence.

It matters how a woman presents herself, in the home, at work or on the streets.

It matters what image she projects to her children.

She Is Clothed With Strength And Dignity and Laughs Without Fear Of The Future

It matters what form her life takes, what shape.

She is capable of adjusting or reversing when necessary.

She is capable; making coverings of tapestry is not a walk in the park.

As the saying goes, that a woman will put her best face forward, a woman is not carved out of hard wood, she is soft tissue, she adjusts.

The Bible says she is a weaker vessel, yet not defined by weaknesses.

She is not wishy-washy. She is strong, bold, and yet soft, a person who feels for others.

How she wears her clothes is a statement of who she is. She cannot wear silk and purple and at the same time surround herself with rugs for character.

She recognises that the land is not enough, unless accompanied by springs of water.

Elegant independence means you are an altogether woman – focussed and deliberate.

Spending time *alone* with God, a woman becomes, elegantly independent.

STEP 14

QUIET INFLUENCE

Life is a great teacher, as is often said.

My thinking is, the happenings in life and the happenings of life will have a lasting effect on any person's life.

What happens in our lives inspires us, for good or bad.

The impact of life sways us in certain directions, encourages certain behaviours.

Life as it happens provides the stimuli that guide us.

All the above, relate to influence the power behind.

Over the past "few" years of my life, I have realised that married women and married man are generally ascribed the other's attributes.

When a woman is married, she is often known "through" her husband.

A husband married to a woman who spends time with God is not afraid or intimidated by her success or eloquence.

Not because this woman cannot, but because this woman does not flaunt her abilities.

This woman is a great supporter, not just of her husband.

She is not known, but *her* husband sits with the elders of the land.

She is joyful, when her husband is happy and content. She is joyful because she knows she is the power behind!

Solomon's statement is loaded with meaning, when he says in **Proverbs 31:23** *Her husband is known in the gates, when he sitteth among the elders of the land.*

This man is known, not of his own, but the husband has inferred respect. This husband is so respected by her wife; the community cannot but just respect him too.

When her husband is seen in the street or the board room, he is seen with her and yet without her.

His demeanour, his clothes, his speech, his everything, speaks his wife. The husband is known when he sits.

David says blessed is the man that sitteth not in the seat of the scornful. This woman is noble; she speaks a word in season.

When the community of elders applaud the man, they are applauding the woman.

She does not seek relevance. She is so into the life of those around her she, like Esther, says, if I perish, I perish, yet she is so impactful she knows she *will not* perish, because she is anchored on God, the invincible God..

In **Esther 2**, Esther knew she could not say anything at the wrong time. She was not a woman in a rush, she was patient, she was prudent, and she was wise.

Esther was a Jew who became queen in a foreign land.

Esther was, as the Bible says, fair and beautiful.

She did not take more than she was comfortable with.

Verse 15 says *she required nothing but what Hegai the king's chamberlain, the keeper of the women, appointed. And Esther obtained favour in the sight of all them that looked upon her.*

She had access to all, but did not take anything that was not appointed her. This was and is a virtue that separates Godly women from the rest.

This was the quality that most endeared Esther to the king, for the Bible says Vashti was also fair to look at, the reason why the king wanted to show her off to *all his princes and his servants; the power of Persia and Media, the nobles and princes of the provinces, being before him:*

This was a gathering of powerful man who reigned *from India even unto Ethiopia, over an hundred and seven and twenty provinces:*

The powerful princes had been celebrating and showing *the riches of his glorious kingdom and the honour of his excellent majesty many days, even an hundred and fourscore days.*

The difference between Esther and Vashti is that Vashti failed to read the writing on the wall.

This was no ordinary time to think in ordinary ways.

The king had with him *both unto great and small* (men), *seven days* (of partying), *in the court of the garden of the king's palace;*

Vashti also failed to understand that her freedoms were in the *royal house which belonged to king Ahasuerus.*

The place was not one where she could do as she wished or would.

Vashti needed to know the art of quiet influence!

This was what Esther could and did. Mordecai was her teacher – an older Jew in a foreign land.

In God Alone

Given that when *the heart of the king was merry with wine*, there was no knowing what he would ask for or do, Vashti needed wisdom that could only come from God.

The chamberlains that the king sent to get Vashti were not the same that the king enquired from, as to what to do with queen Vashti.

The king enquired from *the seven princes of Persia and Media, which saw the king's face, and which sat the first in the kingdom;*

If the king had sought advice from the persons he had sent earlier to invite queen Vashti, perhaps they would have explained her reasoning.

That opportunity did not arise.

There are times, in life, when second chances do not come.

Vashti simply assumed a drunken husband would be the same as when sober.

Women who spend time alone with God would know this; drunken husbands are just that - drunk, whether with wine, or wealth or pride.

Drunken husbands need women who spend time with God, the only true God, who knows the end from the beginning, to match and to manoeuvre.

She Is Clothed With Strength And Dignity and Laughs Without Fear Of The Future

Knowing what to do and when not to contest is prudence.

This was a time when Vashti, if she had known God, would have had greater wisdom.

The king was sitting with the princes of Persia and Media.

Their thinking was different: *Vashti the queen hath not done wrong to the king only, but also to all the princes, and to all the people that are in all the provinces of the king Ahasuerus.*

[17] *For this deed of the queen shall come abroad unto all women, so that they shall despise their husbands in their eyes, when it shall be reported, The king Ahasuerus commanded Vashti the queen to be brought in before him, but she came not.*

[18] *Likewise shall the ladies of Persia and Media say this day unto all the king's princes, which have heard of the deed of the queen. Thus shall there arise too much contempt and wrath.*

Most women would have acted or responded like Vashti did.

Women who spend time with God, in these circumstances, when hearts are merry with whatever, need wisdom that comes from God - quietly influencing for positive outcomes.

She Is Clothed With Strength And Dignity and Laughs Without Fear Of The Future

The princes of Persia and Media have one rule - *let the king give her royal estate unto another that is better than she.*

Such is the world we live in, and only the prudent will survive.

Esther knew what to say and when.

She did not take credit for what was not her idea, but *Esther certified the king thereof in Mordecai's name.*

When the king delegates his responsibilities, as he did to Haman *to do with them* (Jews) *as it seemeth good to thee* (Haman), it takes a woman of faith in her God to stand in faith.

The Bible says *And the king and Haman sat down to drink; but the city Shushan was perplexed.*

Esther was needed, not just to clothe Mordecai at the palace gate, but to petition the king for mercy.

A king who has delegated his authority in crisis times is no king at all – but such a king Esther had to handle.

She could, because she was in the king's palace. She knew where to stand so she could be seen, how to talk so she could be heard.

Esther was not foolish. She knew the stakes were high.

She made conversation with herself and with Mordecai.

She made a decision – a command - *Go, gather together all the Jews that are present in Shushan, and fast ye for me, and neither eat nor drink three days, night or day: I also and my maidens will fast likewise; and so will I go in unto the king, which is not according to the law: and if I perish, I perish.*

Esther did not fast alone, even the non-Jews that attended to her had to fast – she convinced them – somehow, she did!

Esther, to accomplish her mission, she stood at a vantage point on the day. That is wisdom, to know your vantage point – your point of influence.

On the third day she *put on her royal apparel, and stood in the inner court of the king's house, over against the king's house: and the king sat upon his royal throne in the royal house, over against the gate of the house.*

And it was so, when the king saw Esther the queen standing in the court, that she obtained favour in his sight: and the king held out to Esther the golden sceptre that was in his hand. So Esther drew near, and touched the top of the sceptre.

Esther knew protocol. She knew exactly what touching the top of the king's sceptre meant – permission granted.

She Is Clothed With Strength And Dignity and Laughs Without Fear Of The Future

When permission was granted, Esther still did not take anything for granted. Four times to end of the banquet she would ask for permission to speak – what wisdom!

Then said the king unto her, What wilt thou, queen Esther? and what is thy request? it shall be even given thee to the half of the kingdom.

Esther played her cards – the banquet.

Whilst Esther was managing her affairs, Haman's wife, because she did not know God, was inadvertently suggesting a cruel end to her own husband.

Esther "banked" on God, and God did the rest. The Lord God took *sleep* from the king – even from a heathen king.

When we play our part, the Lord does His, for *On that night could not the king sleep, and he commanded to bring the book of records of the chronicles; and they were read before the king.*

²*And it was found written, that Mordecai had told of Bigthana and Teresh, two of the king's chamberlains, the keepers of the door, who sought to lay hand on the king Ahasuerus.*

³*And the king said, What honour and dignity hath been done to Mordecai for this? Then said the king's servants that ministered unto him, There is nothing done for him.*

She Is Clothed With Strength And Dignity and Laughs Without Fear Of The Future

4 And the king said, Who is in the court? Now Haman was come into the outward court of the king's house, to speak unto the king to hang Mordecai on the gallows that he had prepared for him.

5 And the king's servants said unto him, Behold, Haman standeth in the court. And the king said, Let him come in. –

Call it coincidence – but what coincidence?

The woman who spends time with God will say, "my God did".

To this woman, there is no coincidence!

Those that fight against us God will use for our deliverance, for our joy.

Haman's wife gave testimony *If Mordecai be of the seed of the Jews, before whom thou hast begun to fall, thou shalt not prevail against him, but shalt surely fall before him.*

A woman who spends time with God covers her kith and kin.

Like Esther, how could she endure to see evil come to her people, or how could she endure to see the destruction of her kindred?

With quiet influence, opportunity will come, for you to make haste and write to all a note in the king's name, seal it with the king's ring, and send letters by posts on horseback, and riders on mules, camels, and young dromedaries.

Esther, with uncle Mordecai, just did.

And many of the people of the land became Jews; for the fear of the Jews fell upon them – quiet influence!

Who knows, woman, who knows, that you may be where you are, for such a moment as you are in.

As **1 Timothy 4:12** says *"Let no man despise thy youth* (or being a woman)*; but be thou an example of the believers, in word, in conversation, in charity, in spirit, in faith, in purity."*

In short – be bold, but not confrontational.

Let no-one despise you for being a woman.

Looking unto Jesus, the author and finisher of our faith, we will prevail.

A weaker vessel, yes, but never in weakness.

STEP 15

ENTERPRISING

There is no better person in the Bible who can best fit the description – enterprising, than the mother of Moses.

Enterprising is being innovative, inventive, and imaginative, resourceful, adventurous, ingenious, creative and intrepid.

As I looked up the word "intrepid" I got excited about the mother of Moses.

Intrepid, is being fearless, bold, courageous, valiant.

It is being heroic, daring and resolute.

Free Google Dictionary Online

Such a woman was the mother of Moses.

The mother of Moses wove a basket that no crocodile or hippo or snake could touch.

She wove a basket that the waters of the Nile could not sink.

She sold her ideas to herself first and then to her family.

In a way, the mother of Moses delivered baby Moses to Pharaoh's daughter!

Solomon could relate to the mother of Moses and call her enterprising.

Enterprising is profitable, both to the kingdom of God as we serve our God, and to man.

Proverbs 31:24 says, an enterprising woman *maketh fine linen, and selleth it; and delivereth girdles unto the merchant.*

As I relate the mother of Moses to this verse of Proverbs, this chapter becomes an analogy of sorts.

Exodus 2:1-10 says *And there went a man of the house of Levi, and took to wife a daughter of Levi.*

² And the woman conceived, and bare a son: and when she saw him that he was a goodly child, she hid him three months.

³ And when she could no longer hide him, she took for him an ark of bulrushes, and daubed it with slime and with pitch, and put the child therein; and she laid it in the flags by the river's brink.

⁴ And his sister stood afar off, to know what would be done to him

The mother of Moses was innovative.

In God Alone

She lived through hard times. Sons born in the Hebrew community were not living.

The mother of Moses knew she had to do something, perhaps not for all the sons born to Hebrew women at that time, but at least to her own.

Something needed to be done.

An enterprising woman has one huge attribute – she can convince.

Moses' mother convinced herself first - her child was going to live. She went on to convince her husband, then her daughter Miriam, that their son and Miriam's brother, was going to live.

With all ingenuity from his mother, Moses lived three months in his family's house.

Moses' mother knew when and how to let go. She invented. She was a thinker, and probably had sleepless nights thinking how she could pull the plan off.

She was very resourceful. All the attributes of a seller were with the mother of one of the great men of God.

The life of Moses was grace camouflaged by adversity and shaped by circumstance.

Moses grew up in Pharaoh's house.

He did, because his mother would not give up.

The Mother of Moses made, sold and delivered.

As women that spend time with God, we can match this standard.

Our God is the same – He does not change. Who He was in Moses' infancy is who He is today and He still will be the same for our posterity.

We ought to thrive because we know this God – the one that gave plenty of brains to the mother of Moses.

Enterprising needs determination.

It is understood that as long as someone stays idle, the brains take a break.

When human beings start thinking, the brain gains upward momentum and opens up new ideas.

How awesome!

The mother of Moses did not need anyone to tell her that her son was a good child – she knew.

The mother of Moses made. She used her hands. She could not afford to let a neighbour know what her intentions were.

The mother of Moses was sober, and she was motivated.

She was not rushed, she was deliberate.

The mother of Moses was decisive, yet thought through her ideas.

The mother of Moses would not bury her head in the sand.

She must have, with all subtlety, checked around what could float, collected all the materials in a very intelligent way. The future was in her hands.

How could she endure letting go of a child she had nursed for three months, each month bringing her closer to destiny.

How could she endure?

What makes many women complacent is because they do not think beyond themselves. A little comfort there and they remove their thinking cap.

The mother of Moses was so good all her household moved with her. No one panicked, no one talked.

She led by principle, she loved and would only let go when she knew Miriam was watching over Moses.

The mother of Moses trained her children, to read time and understand it, to think, and to rise to the occasion.

Miriam did not panic when she saw Pharaoh's daughter.

Her brother was safe, that's what mattered most.

The Bible does not say whether Miriam's mother had told her what to say, the Bible says Miriam was watching over her brother to see what would become of him.

As Miriam's mother's traits had rubbed onto her, she was not sloppy when the need arose.

Miriam talked to Pharaoh's daughter with the conviction of her mother, and Pharaoh's daughter could only agree.

Their God, your God, my God, was in charge.

The intelligence of Egypt's courts had met the intrepidity of a Hebrew girl.

Moses' mother nursed her child until the age he could be "weaned".

I can imagine the mother of Moses, Miriam, and the rest of the family holding hands to pray for Moses, and for Miriam.

Miriam would follow the basket as it floated in the river, through the reeds, through the sand banks, through the mud, Miriam followed.

The mother of Moses must have been praying, "Lord God Almighty, keep your eyes on my children" whilst waiting for Miriam to bring back the news – Moses is safe.

The mother of Moses had all her wits around her, and so had Miriam, and the rest of the family.

Pharaoh's daughter paid Moses' mother to nurse her own child.

Moses' mother went beyond – she taught Moses so well about who he was such that forty years into the desert Moses could remember how his God spoke – even in the wilderness of Midian.

This is the woman Solomon envisaged. The woman Solomon salutes.

She is clever, she is resourceful. This woman delivers girdles to merchants.

This woman trades fine linen and girdles!

What a combination – of skills.

My search indicated that girdles are strong fibre products.

They cannot be spun on the same weave with fine linen.

When one balances fine linen with girdles, her mindset is unbeatable.

In God Alone

With this woman, both hands work.

Right handed, yes, but the left can work equally well.

This woman has balance. She is stable.

This woman does not stand on one foot. She is well grounded.

This woman can deliver, because she is enterprising.

She Is Clothed With Strength And Dignity and Laughs Without Fear Of The Future

STEP 16

MORAL INTELLIGENCE

Principle, is the foundation, the basis, of morals.

It is ethics, it is standards. Your morality is who you are. It is how your mind and your heart are wired to think and to respond.

Your morals define your decency, your goodness, and your outlook on life.

However, because our morality is different, as we have different backgrounds and upbringing, different expectations and visions, then conflict arises because opinions differ.

Intelligence, on the other hand, in context of this chapter, is cleverness, and it is carefulness.

A morally intelligent woman is therefore clever and careful. She lives on principle.

She says to herself "thou shall not" because she is quite capable.

Clever and careful in thought, in speech, and in actions.

She simply lives "on the hill".

She Is Clothed With Strength And Dignity and Laughs Without Fear Of The Future

In her life, her relationships, she always checks out for the hill advantage, because all the other ground, is sinking sand.

It is the woman that can relate to Paul in **Philippians 4:8**, when Paul says

Finally, brethren, whatsoever things are true, whatsoever things are honest, whatsoever things are just, whatsoever things are pure, whatsoever things are lovely, whatsoever things are of good report; if there be any virtue, and if there be any praise, think on these things.

This is the woman Solomon says in **Proverbs 31:25**

Strength and honour are her clothing; and she shall rejoice in time to come.

This statement is loaded with meaning.

She wears strength and honour. Truth or truthfulness brings honour.

True or truthful means correct, factual and real.

Most women are prone to depart from this virtue because of fear – fear of the outcomes, or the consequences.

I will discuss the three aspects that I have alluded to in this chapter in relation to moral intelligence, which is, thought, speech and actions.

Speech

Speech should be governed by the speaker.

As the statement says, stones will break my bones but words will break my heart.

Because most fear to speak, even truthfully, for fear of breaking another's heart, the world and relationships are now built on lies.

Most would not tell the truth because they fear to hurt a spouse's ego or emotions.

Most would not tell the truth because they fear to hurt relationships.

Most lie because they feel they cannot properly express themselves to be heard in context.

Regardless, it is quite clear and evident that it is when one speaks that they are prone to lie.

In short, to avoid hurting someone's feelings, one keeps quiet.

To avoid society's judgement, one speaks less.

Solomon even says those who speak more are likely to err in their speech, as more words imply greater probability to err or lie.

In God Alone

It is the woman who spends time with God who knows when and how to speak.

She knows what to talk about and to who, as what we say can build bridges or break them.

For greater good, when one decides to speak, they need to be honest.

When honesty is at the core of a conversation, there should be no conflict.

A woman that fears the Lord, spending time alone with God, knows what we say, is the fire that burns.

In other words, there is no point in speaking if one cannot speak their mind honestly.

This brings me to the first aspect, thought.

Thoughts

Speaking is saying out aloud. what one is thinking.

Whilst words can break another, thoughts can break or build the thinker first.

As much as people say what they have thought about, what a person thinks shapes both the kind of speech they will give but also how the owner of the thoughts becomes.

We are all shaped by what we have thought.

That thinking process needs moral intelligence. It is the ability to separate the good from the bad, for personal growth, and more principled output.

That is why David in Psalms says people should speak the truth in their heart.

The Psalmist asks [15] *Lord, who shall abide in thy tabernacle? who shall dwell in thy holy hill?*

[2] *He that walketh uprightly, and worketh righteousness, and speaketh the truth in his heart.*

Because people are so used to flattery, it needs women who spend time with God to break the cycle of dishonest conversations.

It all just needs to be said properly and with a lot of empathy.

Women often do not do justice to each other. Women prefer to outdo each other.

Most women issues cease to be fairly and objectively considered.

Most women issues become biased and hurtful to mostly, other women.

My considered view is, women can only be morally intelligent when chapters one [1] to fifteen [15] are correct, in any woman's life.

One's thoughts and one's speech create their actions.

Actions

As I wrote this chapter, I realised speech seemed to be affected by or to affect both thought and actions.

This is because actions speak.

A lot of women who act strangely are those that have placed themselves in places of disadvantage.

These would, for example, have married married man and become the second or third wife.

These would have taken their education like one of those things, and expecting someone to "look after" them.

These women "work" with hands that have long artificial nails.

Inadvertently, their work does not profit because their effort is limited to the strength of their nails!

This is contrary to what God-fearing women would do, for they are clothed with strength and honour.

Strength is power, it is an asset.

The body already has its limits. Long nails add disadvantage to their work effort.

In God Alone

The actions of this woman are pure. Purity comes with honour. As the Bible says, it is the pure in heart who shall see God.

The principle of life is doing unto others as you would like them to do unto you.

The principles of life are not one directional, they work forwards and backwards.

Notwithstanding, there are some women who are placed in places of disadvantage by circumstance.

Moral intelligence is purity, in thought, in speech and in actions, regardless of your place in society.

Our minds, our bodies, our everything should oose out purity.

Purity demands self-respect, discipline, self-restraint, self-training.

Purity demands that we avoid all things impure, look away if necessary and run away when contact is inevitable.

Our eyes as women, ought to see right, our ears ought to hear no evil. This does not and cannot happen if we do not spend time *alone,* with God.

A woman who seeks to be pure ought to tell herself – "This I will not do".

She Is Clothed With Strength And Dignity and Laughs Without Fear Of The Future

These women know, they understand, they have wisdom, and they are intelligent.

They also know, it is not by might nor by power, but by the Spirit of the Lord.

Moral intelligence gives us access to the things we all love, things that are good and adorable.

Prayerfulness, hope filled songs, Bible texts, Godly conversations, guilt free thoughts and considered actions.

These are the things that bring honour and give strength to the mind and body.

These are the things that build strong bonds and strong relationships.

Surrounding ourselves with carefully considered friends and friendships edify and strengthen.

Honourable friends come from God.

Lovely things cannot be separated from things of good report. Good reports are celebrated.

Reports are a statement of strength and honour.

Reports indicate and reflect how others see you, your physical, mental, spiritual, and social stance in the web of life.

When "they" talk about you, what do they say, and when they gossip about you, how do they feel?

Good reports need consistency of performance. You will be defined by your interactions, your steps and your conversations.

A good report means one is operating above bitterness, above vengeance, above show of power, of opulence, and above the mundane.

Mundane is commonplace. Women that spend time alone with God are not every day everywhere women.

That is why David says the steps of a good man [generic] are ordered by the Lord.

Goodness, strength and honour are not gender sensitive.

Good is good.

A good report does not just come; it does not fall from the sky. You work for a good report.

Moral intelligence needs a lot of brain power.

The morally intelligent woman is celebrated.

She has plenty of self-awareness, of her impact on society.

She knows she is a letter that everyone – husband, children, in laws, her kindred, ought to read.

Hate her or love her, all will love to read her story, her report, for inspiration, for growth.

This woman is pretty inside and pretty outside.

STEP 17

EMOTIONAL INTELLIGENCE

Women are generally regarded as emotional.

Not so fast I say, because most women are emotionally intelligent.

My assertion is based on the definition of emotional.

It is defined as being expressive, passionate and enthusiastic.

They cry when they feel they want to cry, whether it is "ok" to do so or not.

In that cry there is strength to go on; there is a decision for balance.

My observation is, when a woman has not yet cried, happy or sad, that woman would be emotionally unbalanced.

The crying does not need to be public. The crying can be very private.

That emotion, that comes with tears, can be the reasoning behind her intelligence.

When one woman is crying, most cry with her as well.

She Is Clothed With Strength And Dignity and Laughs Without Fear Of The Future

This seems like a contradiction of chapter 16. No, it is not.

Whilst one woman's words may sting another, most would cry with the target when she cries.

More women pray than men, in any setup or environment.

Most women are hinged on their God, because, in a way, they are the burden bears.

Their responsibilities are huge, because the responsibilities are just many.

An unstable woman will not stand the trials and tribulations of child bearing, of keeping the home clean and tidy, of managing diets for the nursing, the children, the elderly and the infirm.

Of necessity, a woman ought to be balanced and thoroughly hinged emotionally.

In that daily "workout" only God can give strength.

In that daily "workout" it would very easy to snap, to break down.

This balanced woman, as in **Proverbs 31:26**, *She openeth her mouth with wisdom; and in her tongue is the law of kindness.*

In this "workout" it is imperative that women be sober and alert.

Alert to other women's vulnerabilities.

Life will happen and no amount of preparedness will stop anything, good or bad, from happening.

What is important is that when life happens, we remain in full control of our faculties.

In the mayhem of life, women cry so that they are understood.

Hannah did. Her soul cried, the depth of her personality cried.

When the priest Elli thought she was drunk – she was operating at a different level – she was consulting heaven over her barrenness.

Women who spend time alone with God, man cannot understand, children marvel and neighbours admire.

In **1 Samuel 1**, Elkanah could not understand his wife – how could she not be happy with a double portion of anything and everything good on offer.

Elkanah did not know what it took for Hannah to stay in the same environs with Penninah.

Hannah's kind of cry, man cannot understand.

In God Alone

Hannah was Godly – she wanted her own, because she was Hannah (favour; grace), she was not a Penninah (precious stone).

Women who spend time with God operate at the level of grace and favour and not on value of exchange.

Their life is faith based; it is not based on vain beauty.

Those with grace and favour do not fight with vain beauty, they are grounded on the word and promises of God.

When Godly women open their mouths to speak, the words are selected well, the speech is measured and the context is kind.

This is where emotional intelligence comes in, that ability to control how one speaks.

Expressively, passionately and enthusiastically, we understand, but how does it leave the other person feeling.

Hannah knew, whatever she did, if she operated at Elkanah and Penninah's level, she would not succeed.

Hannah thought to reason with God.

Hannah spoke so expressively and passionately Elli thought she was drunk.

When you reason with God, in your private space, you are emotionally intelligent.

Women seem emotionally entangled because they want to be comforted, sometimes too publicly!

When you expose your thinking to God and not to man, you are bound to be comforted.

Our God is the God of all comfort.

Our God deals with us at all emotional levels.

The word of God is our intelligence; it goes to the depths of our being.

Paul says to the Hebrews,

12 For the word of God is quick, and powerful, and sharper than any two-edged sword, piercing even to the dividing asunder of soul and spirit, and of the joints and marrow, and is a discerner of the thoughts and intents of the heart.

13 Neither is there any creature that is not manifest in his sight: but all things are naked and opened unto the eyes of him with whom we have to do.

14 Seeing then that we have a great high priest, that is passed into the heavens, Jesus the Son of God, let us hold fast our profession.

In God Alone

15 For we have not an high priest which cannot be touched with the feeling of our infirmities; but was in all points tempted like as we are, yet without sin.

16 Let us therefore come boldly unto the throne of grace, that we may obtain mercy, and find grace to help in time of need **[Hebrews 4:12-16].**

There is a lot of comfort in these verses.

Our everything rests on these Hebrew verses – the quick and powerful word of God, which allows us to come boldly before the throne of God.

The Elkanahs of our lives may never know, that what is so important to us, what makes us shed tears, is not what they think – it's what only God can give – peace.

Samuel was peace to Hannah, for Penninah stopped what she thought, said and did to Hannah, when Samuel was born.

Sometimes it is "our own" which makes the difference.

Whether the other has ten and another two, it does not matter, as long as we have *our own*. Only God can understand that.

Hannah was grace and favour – yet she was barren, and the Lord, her God, had shut up her womb. Hannah knew, only God could reverse. She was

She Is Clothed With Strength And Dignity and Laughs Without Fear Of The Future

In God Alone

seeking God when the priest thought she was on a drunken stupor – what thinking!

The woman who spends time with God communes and talks with God. Better still, alone with her God.

There, she can shed her tears and no one will judge her, because the Lord, her God, knows what each tear drop means.

Pastors and priests are people, whilst God, is God.

Pastors are priests, who can mark your mouth, read your lips but not your heart.

They can think you are drunk and may never know, just how much your God is close to your issues.

Emotional intelligence is talking with God – He does not understand, He knows.

In your situation, anyone else who is not God, will tell you to put away your wine, but God will listen as you pour out your heart to Him.

Hannah says *for out of the abundance of my complaint and grief have I spoken hitherto.*

Hannah said it as it was, to God, and no one else ever knew.

A woman who spends time with God does not desire to be heard by those that cannot help.

She Is Clothed With Strength And Dignity and Laughs Without Fear Of The Future

In God Alone

She is intelligent, even in her grief and complaint.

When you have finished talking with God, you are at peace, you can eat, you are peaceful, you stop crying, you stop complaining, and you stop grieving.

In God and with God, you rest.

Elkanah did not witness these two conversations, between Hannah and her God, and between Hannah and Eli. Elkanah was just not there.

Hannah could name her son Samuel and take him to the temple, because she knew *how* she got her son.

Elkanah could not object, because he did not know how.

Elkannah probably asked, and Hannah probably said – the Lord's mercies never fail, they are new every morning.

Elkanah would never understand, how God could answer Hannah's prayer "just like that".

When a woman stays put with God, she will rejoice in her God.

The crying stopped, because Hannah knew where and how to process her emotions.

She simply went back to God Before Samuel, Hannah prayed, after Samuel she also prayed.

She Is Clothed With Strength And Dignity and Laughs Without Fear Of The Future

And Hannah prayed, and said, My heart rejoiceth in the LORD, mine horn is exalted in the LORD: my mouth is enlarged over mine enemies; because I rejoice in thy salvation.

² There is none holy as the LORD: for there is none beside thee: neither is there any rock like our God.

³ Talk no more so exceeding proudly; let not arrogancy come out of your mouth: for the LORD is a God of knowledge, and by him actions are weighed.

⁴ The bows of the mighty men are broken, and they that stumbled are girded with strength.

⁵ They that were full have hired out themselves for bread; and they that were hungry ceased: so that the barren hath born seven; and she that hath many children is waxed feeble.

⁶ The LORD killeth, and maketh alive: he bringeth down to the grave, and bringeth up.

⁷ The LORD maketh poor, and maketh rich: he bringeth low, and lifteth up.

⁸ He raiseth up the poor out of the dust, and lifteth up the beggar from the dunghill, to set them among princes, and to make them inherit the throne of glory: for the pillars of the earth are the LORD's, and he hath set the world upon them.

⁹ He will keep the feet of his saints, and the wicked shall be silent in darkness; for by strength shall no man prevail.

Hannah's prayer says it all; outside God, we are emotional wrecks.

For by strength shall no man prevail.

We all need God.

STEP 18

STRONG WORK ETHIC

A work ethic is a set of moral principles a person uses in their job.

People who possess a strong work ethic embody certain principles that guide their work behaviour, leading them to produce high-quality work consistently and the output motivates them to stay on track.

https://en.m.wikipedia.org

Working, at times, is not what we want, but what we need.

We need to work for its reward.

Where and how you get your reward then becomes important.

Where and how you work is and should be guided by your principles.

With strong moral principles, nothing beats a just reward.

Just because the reward is from the work of your own hands, your effort and your mind.

Solomon imagines a woman who does not borrow, because she is not and has not been idle.

Proverbs 31:27 says, *She looketh well to the ways of her household, and eateth not the bread of idleness.*

The statement goes – you eat or you reap what you sow.

This Proverbs woman sows hard work and kindness, and she is justly rewarded.

The equation starts with the application of the mind – looking well. Looking is easy. Everyone who has eyes looks.

Even the blind "look" to the direction of the voice. So looking is just that – looking.

There is a difference in the response of one who looks and sees and one who just looks.

Seeing is interpretation, whilst looking ends with a physical presentation.

The one who looks well has a higher level of understanding. She is not just seeing today, she is also seeing tomorrow.

Looking well means discerning or understanding what one is looking at.

As alluded to earlier, a woman has a myriad of responsibilities.

These are the ways of her household, the what and the how.

The ways of doing what you do, is what Solomon is concerned about. It is the question that most do not ask.

The ways of a household are many – some are sloppy, some diligent, some preach cleanliness, some everything goes, some stable and sober, some strong on bonds, some very weak, some gluttonous, some anything and some everything.

If the what and the how are not adequately addressed, yet people still want to eat well, sleep well, travel well, then there is a big challenge – where to get your bread and your water.

Does not eat the bread of idleness comes in two ways -

The first is she refuses to eat what she has not worked for.

The second is she refuses to be associated with what idle people do and talk about.

In short, this woman works, and works within the law.

She is the lady who David says in Psalms 1

Blessed is the man (or woman) *that walketh not in the counsel of the unGodly, nor standeth in the way of sinners, nor sitteth in the seat of the scornful.*

² But his delight is in the law of the LORD; and in his law doth he meditate day and night.

³ And he shall be like a tree planted by the rivers of water, that bringeth forth his fruit in his season; his leaf also shall not wither; and whatsoever he doeth shall prosper.

⁴ The unGodly are not so: but are like the chaff which the wind driveth away.

This woman has no time and place for the unGodly.

Genesis 29:9-14 gives an impression of this woman in this narrative of Rachel.

⁹ While he was still talking with them, Rachel came with her father's sheep, for she was a shepherd. ¹⁰ When Jacob saw Rachel daughter of his uncle Laban, and Laban's sheep, he went over and rolled the stone away from the mouth of the well and watered his uncle's sheep. ¹¹ Then Jacob kissed Rachel and began to weep aloud. ¹² He had told Rachel that he was a relative of her father and a son of Rebekah. So she ran and told her father.

The Bible says Rachel was a shepherd.

What a profession.

Rachel was a woman who understood she needed to be strong physically and mentally.

She needed to "read the mind and understand the language" of the sheep to know if it was ill, thirsty, hurt, everything.

Each day would be different from the last.

The weather would change, the direction of the wind would change – it was huge.

And the sheep were not small in number – it was a significant flock.

Rachel had to account for every single sheep, to herself first and then to her father.

The whole family depended on Rachel's account.

She had to create an environment for the sheep to flourish.

She had to fight predators – she needed to be alert and very sober. She could not sleep.

Rachel's work meant she could not afford to sit idly or even get involved in unproductive conversations.

Work ethic distinguishes households, people and even siblings.

She Is Clothed With Strength And Dignity and Laughs Without Fear Of The Future

Many Christians talk a lot of the differences between Rachel and Leah, and believe it was just the eyes that differentiated them.

I am convinced the work ethic also did.

Jacob saw Rachel working.

A working person has greater confidence, contributes meaningfully to conversation, is alert to issues, asks questions, manages time – a working woman inspires.

Working does not mean being on someone else's payroll – it means doing something that brings benefit into your life, home and community.

Working means behaviour that leads to producing high-quality work consistently.

Working means the output of your labour motivates to do more and to stay on track.

Work ethic does not matter whether male or female.

The two attributes of consistent high-quality work, and staying on track, were also found in Joseph.

Everyone looks for a person with a strong work ethic to employ. Pharaoh did.

In **Genesis 47: 6** Pharaoh says to Joseph;

The land of Egypt is before thee; in the best of the land make thy father and brethren to dwell; in the land of Goshen let them dwell: and if thou knowest any men of activity among them, then make them rulers over my cattle.

Pharaoh asks Joseph to employ *man of activity,* to be rulers over his cattle.

Idleness has no reward, regardless of your circumstances.

Output and reward, are motivators. These come at three levels:

The money level – this is the first level.

This level is where everyone else is operating from.

People look to money to "solve" their day to day problems.

Cattle level – the second level.

This level comes when money as we know it, fails.

The Bible says in Genesis,

And when money failed in the land of Egypt, and in the land of Canaan, all the Egyptians came unto Joseph, and ....Joseph said, give your cattle; and I will give you for your cattle, if money fail. And they brought their cattle unto Joseph: and Joseph gave them bread in exchange for horses, and for the flocks, and for the cattle of the herds, and for the asses: and he fed them with bread for all their cattle for that year.

Land level – the highest and best work level.

Moses goes on to say, in the book of Genesis,

And Joseph bought all the land of Egypt for Pharaoh; for the Egyptians sold every man his field, because the famine prevailed over them: so the land became Pharaoh's.... Only the land of the priests bought he not; for the priests had a portion assigned them of Pharaoh, and did eat their portion which Pharaoh gave them: wherefore they sold not their lands.

What is clear is that at any level of output, we need God.

In Egypt, when the famine was sore, even the prime land of Goshen was sold back to Pharaoh.

No wonder when another Pharaoh came "who did not know Joseph" the Israelites became "prisoners".

They had no land and could not claim an inheritance in Egypt.

A woman who spends time alone with God knows exactly what to do, when and how.

The work ethic should be consistent with what we believe.

Work, at any and all the three levels mentioned in this chapter, brings no guarantees.

However, a strong work ethic always brings hope.

God also works with people who work. God does not work with idle people.

In **2 Kings 4** a narrative is given of a time when money failed, cattle failed and land failed.

Chapter 4 says

Now there cried a certain woman of the wives of the sons of the prophets unto Elisha, saying, Thy servant my husband is dead; and thou knowest that thy servant did fear the LORD: and the creditor is come to take unto him my two sons to be bondmen.

² And Elisha said unto her, What shall I do for thee? tell me, what hast thou in the house? And she said, Thine handmaid hath not anything in the house, save a pot of oil.

³ Then he said, Go, borrow thee vessels abroad of all thy neighbours, even empty vessels; borrow not a few.

⁴ And when thou art come in, thou shalt shut the door upon thee and upon thy sons, and shalt pour out into all those vessels, and thou shalt set aside that which is full.

⁵ So she went from him, and shut the door upon her and upon her sons, who brought the vessels to her; and she poured out.

⁶ *And it came to pass, when the vessels were full, that she said unto her son, Bring me yet a vessel. And he said unto her, There is not a vessel more. And the oil stayed.*

⁷ *Then she came and told the man of God. And he said, Go, sell the oil, and pay thy debt, and live thou and thy children of the rest.*

Elisha's instructions are work instructions.

There is always something in the house, something to work with.

We only need to look a little harder, to understand.

Ready-made does not usually apply to most of what we do in life.

For this widow, the oil was there, but it needed to be worked on for increase.

The lady had to pour it out.

God, being God, could have dropped manna from heaven for the lady and her sons, but no, even in her grieving, she had to work.

When we work, we do not shout out, but our product, our oil, will shout out – consistent high-quality work.

What this lady borrowed were empty jars and the Lord filled them up.

Her second job was to sell what the Lord had blessed so she could live.

The Bible says that God gives power – of mind and body – to get wealth.

Everyone ought to work. Even loving husbands cannot stand idle and lazy women.

Of this, Paul says;

And that ye study to be quiet, and to do your own business, and to work with your own hands, as we commanded you;

12 That ye may walk honestly toward them that are without, and that ye may have lack of nothing **[1Thessalonians 4:11].**

STEP 19

GRATEFUL

There are instances in life when some people have said they do not know what they should be grateful for.

My mind was puzzled, because life in itself, the ability to breathe, is the best blessing.

When you are not yet dead then you can be hopeful.

Some have said they are grateful for blessings.

Some have said they count their blessings, and when they do, then they are grateful.

I have wondered, at what number does one then start being grateful for the blessings counted.

Which blessing does one start with and where do they end.

Is there then a hierarchy of or to blessings, so we know when and when not to be grateful?

Or is being grateful the same as counting your blessings?

And can you really count the blessings?

At what stage or age do we then stop counting?

She Is Clothed With Strength And Dignity and Laughs Without Fear Of The Future

In my mind, counting is maths.

Godly things are not mathematical, Godly things are qualitative and infinite I believe.

Being grateful should be our state of being.

Solomon says the children and the husband of a woman who spends time with God are grateful. So is she.

Solomon says in **Proverbs 31:28**

Her children arise up, and call her blessed; her husband also, and he praiseth her.

Where there is God everyone is grateful – one for and to another.

I prefer to "count" my blessings as one big whole – the grace of God – too big, too deep, too wide to count.

First John 3:1 which says

Behold, what manner of love the Father hath bestowed upon us, that we should be called the sons of God: therefore the world knoweth us not, because it knew him not.

This word is beautiful to grateful hearts.

It means grace to be protected, grace to be healed, grace to be satisfied, grace to be saved.

In God Alone

The love and the loveliness of God is the ultimate blessing.

Love cannot be counted, even between man and woman, between parent and child, and between friends.

The Merriam-Webster dictionary says a blessing is the act or words of one that blesses or a thing conducive to happiness or good welfare.

We cannot begin to think what blessings and single them out one by one – we run the risk of forgetting some and failing to thank God for such.

From Genesis, God blessed birds, animals and human beings - be fruitful and multiply.

Right up to Revelation, the Lord says blessed is the man who dies in Christ.

David says blessed is the man whose sins are forgiven.

The Bible says in Isaiah

²*When thou pass through the waters, I will be with thee; and through the rivers, they shall not overflow thee: when thou walk through the fire, thou shalt not be burned; neither shall the flame kindle upon thee.*

³ *For I am the* LORD *thy God, the Holy One of Israel, thy Saviour: I gave Egypt for thy ransom, Ethiopia and Seba for thee* **[Isaiah 43:2-3]**.

The blessings list in these verses cannot be counted.

This scripture means the Lord can pay ransom for Godliness, all the land of Egypt and Seba, and everything in them.

David then says, if it were not for the Lord.

David must have thought far and wide, from Saul to Absalom, and realised only God gave a blessing – of deliverance.

David must have also thought of all the wealth God gave – and realised, only God could have given.

David thought of the time he was sick and sickly, but prayed. He knew, only God could have healed.

The Psalmist says in **Psalms 124** *If it had not been the* LORD *who was on our side, now may Israel say;*

² *If it had not been the* LORD *who was on our side, when men rose up against us:*

³ *Then they had swallowed us up quick, when their wrath was kindled against us:*

4 Then the waters had overwhelmed us, the stream had gone over our soul:5 Then the proud waters had gone over our soul.

The situation was dire - proud waters were raging waters, a torrent, incessant.

Life was happening.

Streams of troubles, of disease, of poverty, can be strong.

Out of such, one should be grateful, for the Lord our God knows, sees and delivers.

Delivery does not just come, you call and the Lord delivers.

Psalms 50:15 says when we are delivered, we praise God.

Praising God is being grateful.

Isaiah 59:19 also says

So shall they fear the name of the LORD from the west, and his glory from the rising of the sun. When the enemy shall come in like a flood, the Spirit of the LORD shall lift up a standard against him.

That type of blessing no one can count.

In God Alone

The blessing to wake up is a loaded blessing. We sleep not just physically, but spiritually, emotionally, mentally and socially.

Only God can wake us up.

We make stupid decisions and only God covers us.

At times we are so out of sorts such that neighbours and all ask how come we are sleeping that way.

Gratefulness says "if it were not for the mercies of God".

We all start the journey of a thousand miles, but not all of us get there.

Life can happen after that single step, and some fall by the way side.

When you walk and get there, wherever that is, that is grace.

Some think to take a nap and never wake up.

Grateful we ought to be – that we are awake to everything that we see and understand.

We cannot put a number to the blessing that we should be grateful for.

We cannot say waking up from a physical sleep is number 1, or going to work is blessing number 9, or the breath of life is number 940.

As women who spend time with God, we can only praise. That applause, is being grateful.

That is why David says, let everything that has breath praise the Lord, and in

Praise ye the LORD. Praise, O ye servants of the LORD, praise the name of the LORD.² Blessed be the name of the LORD from this time forth and for evermore.³ From the rising of the sun unto the going down of the same the LORD's name is to be praised....⁵ Who is like unto the LORD our God, who dwelleth on high,..⁷He raiseth up the poor out of the dust, and lifteth the needy out of the dunghill;⁸ That he may set him with princes, even with the princes of his people.⁹ He maketh the barren woman to keep house, and to be a joyful mother of children. Praise ye the LORD **[Psalms 113].**

The blessings we receive and have received from the Lord are beyond our capacity to count.

We just need grateful hearts.

In God Alone

Our speech, our thoughts, our actions should show that we are truly grateful to God for all He has done for us as His children.

The story of the blessings we received and receive from God is a story that never ends.

For everything, we are grateful.

Grateful, not to man, but to God.

STEP 20

UNPARALLELED INTERGRITY

Integrity, as I was growing up, seemed a very big word.

It still is.

Two definitions of integrity resonate with me are; uprightness and honour.

These are great words, and great women know these two words.

Great women understand uprightness, they understand honour.

Honour and uprightness belong to God. They define Godliness.

Great women, who spend time alone with God, know how to distinguish themselves.

To be great means you operate at a higher level.

The Shunamite woman was one of them.

This is the woman Solomon can say of in **Proverbs 31:29**

Many daughters have done virtuously, but thou excellest them all.

This woman had no comparison. She was above reproach.

There was no appearance of evil around her. She came highly commended.

The heart of her husband was at peace. When she left the home for errands, the husband knew he had nothing to fear.

This woman learnt of God and lived by that knowledge.

Women who are called by the name of the Lord ought to be this virtuous – excellent.

From **2 Kings 4:8**

And it fell on a day, that Elisha passed to Shunem, where was a great woman; and she constrained him to eat bread. And so it was, that as oft as he passed by, he turned in thither to eat bread.

This lady could "read" people. She could separate the good from the bad.

The Bible does not tell us how Elisha got to pass through her home.

What the Bible says is Elisha passed through Shumen.

Shunem was a place, a village or town. In that town or village, then lived a great woman.

This woman must have been known in the village, and Elisha probably passed to Shunem to see her.

Elisha's first encounter with the woman established a lasting relationship – as often as he passed by, he turned in the home of the woman to eat bread.

This woman had a family. She was married.

The husband to this woman is not even talked about for much of the story.

The great Shunamite woman is the one that perceives, notices, and acknowledges that Elisha was a man of God.

The Bible says

And she said unto her husband, Behold now, I perceive that this is an holy man of God, which passeth by us continually.

10 Let us make a little chamber, I pray thee, on the wall; and let us set for him there a bed, and a table, and a stool, and a candlestick: and it shall be, when he cometh to us, that he shall turn in thither.

The discussion with her husband is unassuming. She has a great idea, but she also knew there were limits.

Going together was better than going alone. She said *let us*.

She probably could have done all herself – it was going to be a little chamber on an existing wall, a bed, a table, a stool and a candle stick, but she sought the involvement of her husband.

Her husband knew his wife, under scrutiny, she would not fail.

This woman's integrity kept her at the door.

The Bible says

And when he had called her, she stood in the door.

This was when Elisha told her about the child. She was keenly aware and alert - avoid, look away and run.

Avoid any appearance of evil. Perception is reality.

Integrity differentiates.

My thinking is, going inside and standing at the door are very different positions.

When Elisha promised a child to this couple, the husband was not there. He believed his wife's statement – it had to be correct.

She is one-woman Solomon could also say her husband trusts her – to do him good all her days.

She Is Clothed With Strength And Dignity and Laughs Without Fear Of The Future

When the child that had been born to the couple died, the husband instructed *Carry him to his mother.*

This verse ¹⁹ *And he said unto his father, My head, my head. And he said to a lad, Carry him to his mother* is a chapter on its own.

He knew the mother would do the right thing. This woman was great.

There is simply no greatness if there is no God.

The great woman had a greater husband.

When his wife asks to take their son to Elisha,

²³ *he said, wherefore wilt thou go to him to day? it is neither new moon, nor sabbath. And she said, It shall be well.*

This woman spent time with God, at the new moon and on Sabbath.

The husband knew this and was not in doubt; the woman could go alone and still be ok.

Assured that all was going to be well, he loaded her with what she needed and let her be.

Great was the woman but greater was the husband.

The Bible says

²⁴ *Then she saddled an ass, and said to her servant, Drive, and go forward; slack not thy riding for me, except I bid thee.*

The lady had servants who understood her, fair and firm.

When she said "drive, go forward and slack not", they did.

Elisha also saw and recognized the great woman of Shunem, from a distance.

This woman could not be mistaken, even from a distance.

She was not an everywhere present woman. That is why Elisha was surprised when she rode over.

Where she was, there has to be some mission.

Elisha gives instruction to his servant to run and meet her. Elisha knew something was amiss.

This woman is not all over the place. She is at the right place at the right time.

It was not the new moon and it was not the Sabbath. Someone had to run.

The Bible says Elisha said to Gehazi

²⁶Run now, I pray thee, to meet her, and say unto her, Is it well with thee? is it well with thy husband? is it well with the child? And she answered, It is well.

The great woman was consistent – Gehazi was not Elisha.

She would tell her story to the right person, one who could help. The one who prayed and God heard.

Great women are not all over the place, telling their story to any who would listen.

Great women tell God because it is only God who can help. The death of a son is not small issue; it requires the Giver of Life.

Great women know the rules: -

For the Lord gives wisdom; from his mouth come knowledge and understanding; he stores up sound wisdom for the upright; he is a shield to those who walk in integrity, guarding the paths of justice and watching over the way of his saints **[Proverbs 2:6-8].**

Whoever walks in integrity walks securely, but he who makes his ways crooked will be found out **[Proverbs 10:9].**

The integrity of the upright guides them, but the crookedness of the treacherous destroys them **[Proverbs 11:3].**

She Is Clothed With Strength And Dignity and Laughs Without Fear Of The Future

In God Alone

Women talk about selling tomatoes, sewing and baking.

There are issues which only God can address, issues which, even husbands, cannot understand.

When a child dies, only God should hear.

When love is lost, God wins us back, to love and to be loved again.

When faith is challenged, God builds it back.

When hope is lost, God gives it back.

When we have lost ground, anyway anytime, God gains it back for us.

When the foundations are shaken, God has the answers.

God does not talk you over it, He restores.

27And when she came to the man of God to the hill, she caught him by the feet: but Gehazi came near to thrust her away. And the man of God said, Let her alone; for her soul is vexed within her: and the LORD hath hid it from me, and hath not told me.

The whole way, this woman did not throw herself around in mourning, she did not.

She Is Clothed With Strength And Dignity and Laughs Without Fear Of The Future

In God Alone

She opened up what was whirling up inside her at the door of the man of God.

God hid the story to Elisha, because God wanted the great woman to tell her story.

The Lord could have told Elisha that the woman was coming and what Elisha ought to do. But the Lord never did.

Gehazi could not read that this episode was different.

This woman was already there, on top of the hill.

She knew, she believed and she prayed:

¹I will lift up mine eyes unto the hills, from whence cometh my help. ² My help cometh from the LORD, which made heaven and earth. ³ He will not suffer thy foot to be moved: he that keepeth thee will not slumber.⁴ Behold, he that keepeth Israel shall neither slumber nor sleep.⁵ The LORD is thy keeper: the LORD is thy shade upon thy right hand.⁶ The sun shall not smite thee by day, nor the moon by night. ⁷ The LORD shall preserve thee from all evil: he shall preserve thy soul. ⁸ The LORD shall preserve thy going out and thy coming in from this time forth, and even for evermore.

The husband had been correct – take the boy to her mother!

The woman held Elisha's feet and would not let go.

The servant Gehazi could not read the language of pain, of anguish.

There will be people that great women will come across, who profess knowledge of God but are far from God's discerning, healing and restoring power.

Great women know them, they understand them.

You should never share the death issues with them, because there is nothing they can do to help, other than talk about it.

Great women know where to run, when there is death in the family.

They know when to slow down and when to run.

Hold on to your faith, your answer is right there, at the feet of Jesus, the cross, at Calvary, at Mount Zion, the mountain of God.

Faith does not make it easy, it makes it possible.

When you do keep your faith and your integrity, you will not be disappointed.

God does not disappoint.

STEP 21

SELF-SACRIFICING HUMILITY

As I have been writing, I realised definitions matter, because words do not always mean the same thing.

I will start by defining self.

A definition from Oxford languages says

Self means "a person's essential being that distinguishes them from others, especially considered as the object of introspection or reflexive action".

This means we are different, as different as our finger prints.

In that case, self has to be aware of what distinguishes self from the next person.

When that happens, life can be shared, without one person owing another.

Sharing becomes mutual, because our strengths and weaknesses are different.

Regardless, there are some who are more endowed with significant attributes than others.

Where one is weak, another is strong.

She Is Clothed With Strength And Dignity and Laughs Without Fear Of The Future

Those differences should be the reason for collaboration, for working together, for empathy, for compassion.

Those with more only got more because they received favour from the Lord.

The only favour a woman who spends time with God will seek is favour from the Lord.

Favour received from any other source is a cost.

Favour is often shrouded in mystery because it is favour.

It is not deserved, it is not accounted to the person receiving it, it is not earned, it is a gift.

The second word is sacrificing.

Sacrificing is offering.

A woman who spends time alone with God knows she is not any better than the next person, because we are all short, in one way or the other.

Lending a hand will not mean superiority; it only means I am stronger where you are weaker, not weak.

What she offers is not offered as favour given, by man to man, or woman to woman, or whatever else combination of links there may be.

What is offered should be done in humility.

It is not a gift, for a gift goes before another.

Gifts are given in expectation of a future return.

A gift from a human being is no gift. It is either a return from an earlier "transaction" or a forward payment for anticipated payment to giver, at some future time.

This is why Solomon says favour is deceitful.

It gives an impression of camaraderie – that things are ok. You and I are friends.

There is just one friend in this world – the one that Solomon says sticks closer than a brother.

The friend is Jesus the son of the most high God, the Creator of the Universe, the Giver of Life.

Solomon says in **Proverbs 31:30**

Favour is deceitful, and beauty is vain: but a woman that feareth the LORD, she shall be greatly and continually praised.

Solomon took favour at another level. He says favour deceives.

When you hold yourself because of what you received, then you are living in deceit, deceiving yourself.

In God Alone

A woman who spends time with God cannot lose sleep for favour, neither is she absorbed with beauty.

Because beauty is vain – it has been the Achilles hill for many women.

David says

For the Lord God is a sun and shield; the Lord bestows favour and honour. No good thing does he withhold from those who walk uprightly **[Psalm 84:11].**

Women look themselves in the mirror and think looks are more than that. No, they are not. Looks are just that – looks.

It is how you look at yourself that creates to you a picture of yourself.

What David says resonates with what Solomon said.

An upright woman is greatly and continually praised.

An upright person is humble. These women do not need favours from man, because they are favoured by God, the Creator of the Universe, the Giver of Life.

They do all, in fear of the Lord.

When you fear the Lord, you do not fear retribution – you fear to hurt those the Lord loves.

They are humble.

She Is Clothed With Strength And Dignity and Laughs Without Fear Of The Future

They do all in humility, not "overemphasising" their capabilities.

They know, all they have, is favour.

Knowing this, is wisdom.

Women that spend time with God know that the fear of the Lord is the beginning of wisdom.

They fear to hurt those Jesus died for. They fear to take light of Calvary.

When you fear the Lord, you follow Christ. Your standard is Jesus, your reaction to life and its challenges is Christ centred.

They lean from Jesus, meek and lowly in heart.

Paul in **Romans 16** says

I commend unto you Phebe our sister, which is a servant of the church which is at Cenchrea:

² That ye receive her in the Lord, as becometh saints, and that ye assist her in whatsoever business she hath need of you: for she hath been a succourer of many, and of myself also.

³ Greet Priscilla and Aquila my helpers in Christ Jesus:

4 Who have for my life laid down their own necks: unto whom not only I give thanks, but also all the churches of the Gentiles.

The verses above are not many, but are loaded with meaning.

These women did not beat their drums. They simply feared the Lord.

The ladies knew, favour or beauty, whichever they had, was not anything to write home about.

That is why Paul says

7 For who maketh thee to differ from another? and what hast thou that thou didst not receive? now if thou didst receive it, why dost thou glory, as if thou hadst not received it? **[1 Corinthians 4:7]**.

Paul says they laid down their necks not just for Paul but also for all the churches of the gentiles.

They went out of their way to help the cause of the gospel of Christ. When they did, they did not shout about it.

We do not know their background, but we know they touched every church to which Paul preached in the lands of the gentiles.

There are times we need to put our heads on the block for the Church of God, for our children, for our kith and kin, for our husbands, for everyone – for the sake of the gospel, especially in the churches of the gentiles.

God ought to be seen in our conduct. As the adage says, action speaks louder than words.

Marginalised communities are around us every day.

Sometimes we play the blame game, insisting it is someone's fault.

Sometimes we play the high-end game – we just do not care, as long as we are happy.

We are each other's keeper – who knows – this may be just your time. Phebe does not appear to have had it all.

Paul says help her, but at the same time Paul says she has been a servant of the Church and helped many.

The issue is not whether or not you have anything substantial – its willingness to part with what you have for the benefit of others in greater need.

All human beings, at some point in time, are in need – physical, spiritual, emotional, and mental.

We need someone at a higher level than us in our area of need to stretch a hand, give an ear, take time to pray, or just give us a hug.

Women that spend time with God can never be proud.

They know if it were not for the Lord's mercies…

They are humble.

They have no sense of achievement.

They have self-sacrificing humility. They do what they have to do, not in condescending manner, but in humility.

They fear the Lord, and they shall be praised.

STEP 22

POWERFUL SENSE OF SELF

The woman identified and described by Solomon from verses 10 to 30 is summarised in verse 31.

In that last verse of **Proverbs 31**, Solomon makes a bold statement – give her of the fruit of her hands.

Solomon is sure this lady has something in her hands.

She has sustainable fruit and her works praise her.

Really – her works speak for her.

When you talk about this lady you cannot miss anything, all is there.

High morals, hard work, ability to think things through, mental alertness, good deportment, everything.

Her works praise her.

It is not what others say about you, it is what you say about yourself to you and to others. Your works tell your story.

How you present yourself, how you talk, how you think tells who you are.

She Is Clothed With Strength And Dignity and Laughs Without Fear Of The Future

Solomon says in **Proverbs 31:31**

Give her of the fruit of her hands; and let her own works praise her in the gates.

Within your community your works will talk about you.

Nature and humanity will confederate to give this woman, the fruit of her hand.

Nay sayers will always be there, but her works will speak for her, to confound the negativity of enemies and foes.

This implies all our words, all our actions are our investment.

We take out what we put in.

How you look at yourself determines what you put in, and invariably, what you take out.

The language of your works is either positive or negative. It is what you put in that you will take out.

In **Numbers 27** we read about the daughters of Zelophehad – girls with a very high sense of self.

They knew exactly where they stood in the congregation of Israel.

These girls knew the protocol and they knew the law.

In God Alone

These girls knew their God.

The Bible says

Then came the daughters of Zelophehad, the son of Hepher, the son of Gilead, the son of Machir, the son of Manasseh, of the families of Manasseh the son of Joseph: and these are the names of his daughters; Mahlah, Noah, and Hoglah, and Milcah, and Tirzah.

These daughters knew that Joseph was their great grandfather.

There was no way they could come to Canaan and fail to get an inheritance – whether they were girl or boy.

They had a way of thinking that was not common.

They were not timid.

Timidity is a simple reflection of what and how you think and look at yourself.

If you take time with God, you know you have no duplicate – it is you and you alone.

If the world was empty and it was only you on planet earth, Jesus would have still come down for you.

You are priceless, a child of God.

As Paul says

For God hath not given us the spirit of fear; but of power, and of love, and of a sound mind **[2 Timothy 1:70]**.

These five ladies had a very sound mind.

Solomon wrote years after these ladies were dead, but appreciates women who have time alone with their God.

Solomon says,

For the LORD will be your confidence, and will keep your foot from being caught **[Proverbs 3:26]**.

The Lord was their confidence.

These five girls, the Bible says

² *And they stood before Moses, and before Eleazar the priest, and before the princes and all the congregation, by the door of the tabernacle of the congregation, saying,*

Moses was a great man, and so were the priests, and so large was the congregation of Israel.

The daughters of Zelophehad had a higher understanding of what and who they represented – a whole branch of the family of Joseph.

These ladies were eloquent.

These ladies were brave.

They were full of wisdom.

They were intelligent.

They had a powerful sense of self.

Their approach to the matter was direct, making clear their right to their claim – *our father.*

Something passed on from your father belongs to you. No one else can claim it.

We got a claim – we are called sons [and daughters] of God.

There is no higher claim, none more honourable.

Their second line of thinking was

He [our father] was not in the company of them that gathered themselves together against the LORD in the company of Korah.

These girls knew the goings on in the camp of Israel; they knew what happened when, why and how.

These girls were alert to the issues that mattered.

They were clear in their thinking – our father was not in the company that fell out of favour with God in Korah's day.

They also knew, inheritance was not based on who said what at the edges of Canaan fourty years earlier.

The criterion was clear – state your identity.

Where you got to stay was determined by your tribe, but it was still Canaan.

The Lord's instruction was not gender based – it was birth. Who was your father?

They did not seek a shareholding outside of the norm – they wanted a *possession among the brethren of our father.*

The Bible records their presentation

Our father died in the wilderness, and he was not in the company of them that gathered themselves together against the LORD in the company of Korah; but died in his own sin, and had no sons.

4 Why should the name of our father be done away from among his family, because he hath no son? Give unto us therefore a possession among the brethren of our father.

Whilst these ladies were presenting their case, the all-seeing God watched – five girls against the whole congregation of Israel!

5 And Moses brought their cause before the LORD.

6 And the LORD spake unto Moses, saying,

⁷ The daughters of Zelophehad speak right: thou shalt surely give them a possession of an inheritance among their father's brethren; and thou shalt cause the inheritance of their father to pass unto them.

How would Moses not have known?

What did the congregation think of the daughters of Zelophehad before God made His statement?

God's answer to Moses was very simple, regardless,

⁷ The daughters of Zelophehad speak right.

Amazing God.

The Lord knew whose daughters these girls were.

God called their father by name.

The Bible does not tell us if Moses introduced the girls to God – but we know our God is the Creator of the Universe, He owns everything and knows everyone.

Our God is the Former of All Things.

And God says the girls are right!

God also makes a "new" law!

⁸ And thou shalt speak unto the children of Israel, saying, If a man die, and have no son, then ye shall cause his inheritance to pass unto his daughter.

Our God acknowledges our views too – as women.

Only if we spend time with Him and by Him.

We will know what we ought to say, when, how and to whom.

Godly women do not speak for the sake of speaking.

When they speak, their words are full of wisdom and edify.

Cheap talk is cheap and a woman with a powerful sense of self speaks substance – she is her father's daughter!

CONCLUSION

QUEEN OF THE SOUTH

The woman, who is the subject of this book, may not have it all, but she is altogether.

As mentioned earlier in this book, we will never have enough of what we need or want, but we will all have something to work with, when we share.

This woman is purposeful. She is clear in her mind what she wants.

She lives on principles, she is grounded.

To this lady, Godliness is not a concept, it is life.

As I wrote this book, I kept thinking, which of the Bible mentioned women could have been an altogether woman.

I settled for the Queen of Sheba, queen of the south.

She does not take much of Bible space, yet she got an acknowledgement from Jesus.

Jesus says of her in **Matthew 12:42**,

The queen of the south shall rise up in the judgment with this generation, and shall condemn it: for she came from the uttermost parts of the earth to hear the wisdom of Solomon; and, behold, a greater than Solomon is here.

This woman was awesome.

This woman knew of Adam in Genesis, and of Noah.

She knew of Abraham, Isaac and Jacob.

She knew of Joseph, of Moses, of the judges and kings of Israel.

The queen of Sheba would not know of the many prophets God sent to the children of Israel, so that these children could come back to their God.

This woman would not know Jesus, yet Jesus knew her.

She had no religious dynasty to talk about, she did not belong to the house of Abraham, Isaac or Jacob. If she did, the Bible has hidden that direct link to the patriarchs.

This woman came from the south, according to the medieval Ethiopian work by Kebra Nagast, Sheba was located in Ethiopia.

This place Jesus calls *the uttermost parts of the earth* according to Mathew.

When she *heard of the fame of Solomon concerning the name of the LORD*, she got interested.

In God Alone

It was never about the money.

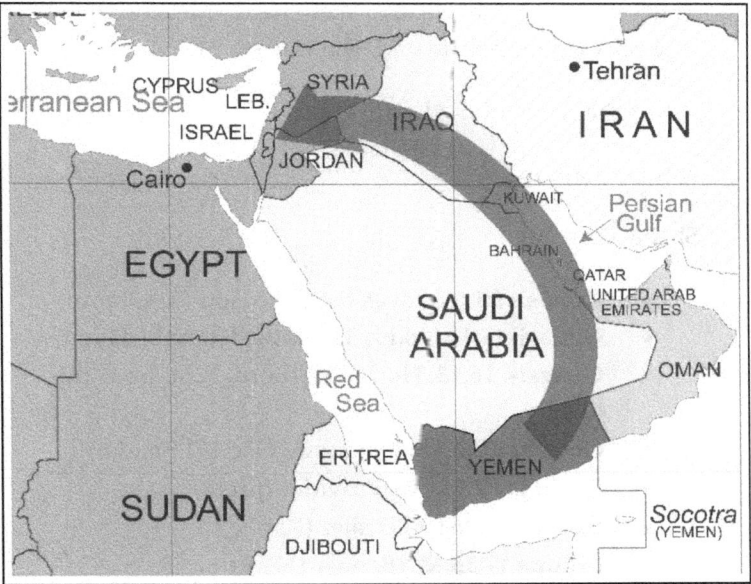

Sheba was rich by her own right.

The queen of Sheba moved because of Solomon's fame concerning the name of the Lord.

The queen knew something about God.

In **1 Kings 10**, the Bible says

10 And when the queen of Sheba heard of the fame of Solomon concerning the name of the LORD, she came to prove him with hard questions.

Sheba travelled a very long distance to see Solomon.

The Bible says the queen asked hard questions. She herself was not intimidated, she was smart.

It was the name of the Lord.

Names matter.

Sheba knew, in

- **Genesis1:1** God was the True God (El-Ohim)
- **Genesis14:19** God is The Most High (El-Elyon)
- **Genesis 16:13** He is The Lord Who Sees (El-Roi)
- **Genesis 17:1** The Almighty God (El-Shadai)
- **Genesis 22:14** The Provider (Jireh)
- **Exodus 15:26** The Healer (Rapha)
- **Exodus 17:15** My Banner (Nissi)
- **Judges 6:24** My Peace (Shalom)
- **Psalms 23:1** My Shepherd (Raah)
- **Jeremiah 23:6** My Righteousness (Tsidken)
- **Ezekiel 38:45** Who Is There (Shamah)
- **Revelation 1:8** The Beginning and the End (Alpha and Omega)

Which name, Sheba must have asked, which made the difference.

Solomon must have answered "I am who I am".

Our God will be who He will choose to be, to meet us as we meet Him.

The woman who spends time with God also knows; as Jeremiah says

"The portion of Jacob is not like them: for He is the former of all things; and Israel is the rod of his inheritance:
The LORD of hosts is his name" **[Jeremiah 10:16 and also Jeremiah 51:19].**

This is what Sheba wanted to enquire about.

These are the hard questions Sheba asked Solomon.

Sheba wanted to know more about this God; she wanted to spend time with such a God.

Jesus acknowledges this desire in Sheba when Jesus says in **Matthew 12:42,**

The queen of the south shall rise up in the judgment with this generation, and shall condemn it: for she came from the uttermost parts of the earth to hear the wisdom of Solomon; and, behold, a greater than Solomon is here.

Jesus statement says "I am here".

If the queen of the south, Sheba, had been around during the time Jesus walked this earth – what would she have done.

In God Alone

Isaiah 47:4 says, *Our Redeemer--the LORD of Hosts is His name--is the Holy One of Israel.*

What would the queen of Sheba had done – knowing that the same Jesus, was the son of God, the same God she sought to know about in Solomon's time.

Sheba would not have asked questions – she would have followed, because Jesus *is greater* than Solomon.

We are talking Jesus the Christ, the son of the Living God, the Creator of the Universe, the Giver of Life.

She did not need to seek permission to go and enquire on the things of God.

She Is Clothed With Strength And Dignity and Laughs Without Fear Of The Future

In God Alone

I will not speculate about her marriage. I just know, she was a woman, like all the women that I know, like me.

She did not have everything, because she asked of Solomon too, but she was an altogether woman.

What she did she did from her endowment.

This woman was a power to reckon with. She was in charge of a kingdom, an empire.

She was complete, with her fears, her faith, her gifts, her talents, her scars, everything.

She wanted answers from Solomon, about her trials, her doubts, her situations and her circumstances.

She says "I did not believe until I had come and seen with my own eyes".

The Bible says

² And she came to Jerusalem with a very great train, with camels that bare spices, and very much gold, and precious stones: and when she was come to Solomon, she communed with him of all that was in her heart.

³ And Solomon told her all her questions: there was not anything hid from the king, which he told her not.

Sheba's heart yearned for God.

She Is Clothed With Strength And Dignity and Laughs Without Fear Of The Future

In God Alone

The Bible says in verse 4

And when the queen of Sheba had seen all Solomon's wisdom, and the house that he had built,

⁵ And the meat of his table, and the sitting of his servants, and the attendance of his ministers, and their apparel, and his cupbearers, and his ascent by which he went up unto the house of the LORD; there was no more spirit in her.

⁶ And she said to the king, It was a true report that I heard in mine own land of thy acts and of thy wisdom,

It was what Sheba saw that put out all the doubt.

She says

⁷ Howbeit I believed not the words, until I came, and mine eyes had seen it: and, behold, the half was not told me: thy wisdom and prosperity exceedeth the fame which I heard.

The queen of the south gave the king of the north presents – from gold to spices, some of which king Solomon and any other king thereafter, has never received.

This was the queen of the south.

She understood, in God alone…

> In Christ alone my hope is found
> He is my light, my strength, my song
> This Cornerstone, this solid ground
> Firm through the fiercest drought and storm

She Is Clothed With Strength And Dignity and Laughs Without Fear Of The Future

In God Alone

What heights of love, what depths of peace
When fears are stilled, when strivings cease
My Comforter, my All in All
Here in the love of Christ I stand

In Christ alone, who took on flesh
Fullness of God in helpless Babe
This gift of love and righteousness
Scorned by the ones He came to save

Till on that cross as Jesus died
The love of God was satisfied
For every sin on Him was laid
Here in the death of Christ I live

There in the ground His body lay
Light of the world by darkness slain
Then bursting forth in glorious Day
Up from the grave He rose again

And as He stands in victory
Sin's curse has lost its grip on me
For I am His and He is mine
Bought with the precious blood of Christ

No guilt in life, no fear in death
This is the power of Christ in me
From life's first cry to final breath
Jesus commands my destiny

No power of hell, no scheme of man
Can ever pluck me from His hand
Till He returns or calls me home
Here in the power of Christ I will stand

On Christ the solid rock I stand
All other ground is sinking sand

She Is Clothed With Strength And Dignity and Laughs Without Fear Of The Future

In God Alone

All other ground, all other ground
Is sinking sand

In Christ Alone (with Stuart Townsend, Julian Keith and
https://www.bing.com/ck/a

REFERENCES

All synonyms – Oxford Dictionary of Languages [Online].

Shipping Guides Ltd. (2018). *Vessel Types Explained*. [online]. Available at: www.portinfo.co.uk/portinformation/ourmaritimeblog/vessel-types-explained [Accessed June 2018]

Wikipedia.org. (2018). *Distaff*. [online]. Available at: https://en.wikipedia.org/wiki/Distaff [Accessed July 11, 2018]

Colourmeanings.com. *Purple Colour Meaning*. [online]. Available at: www.colour-meanings.com/purple-colour-meaning-the-colour-purple/ [Accessed July 10, 2018]

WikiHow.com. *How to make a tent*. [online]. Available at: https://www.wikihow.com/Make-a-Tent [Accessed July 10, 2018]

Irish Studio. (2018). *Florence Nightingale*. [online]. Available at: https://britishheritage.com/florence-nightingale/ [Accessed July 16, 2018]

Wikipedia.org. *Florence Nightingale Ethiopian work Kebra Nagast - Sheba location - (Wikipedia)*. [online]. Available at: https://en.wikipedia.org/wiki/Florence_Nightingale EthiopianworkKebraNagast - Sheba location - (Wikipedia). [Accessed July 16, 2018]

Google.com. (2018). *The Judges of Israel*. [online]. Available at: www.google.co.zw/search?q=judges+of+israel+chart&rlz=1C1CHNY_enZW697ZW701&tbm=isch&tbo=u&source=univ&sa=X&ved=0ahUKEwiMv-vLX_M_bAhVEJsAKHdmsB0gQ7AkIdA&biw=1366&bih=662#imgrc=UI98N9Qu0jErpM [Accessed June 2018]

Definitions - https://en.m.wikipedia.org [online]

www.ingramcontent.com/pod-product-compliance
Lightning Source LLC
Chambersburg PA
CBHW071305110426
42743CB00042B/1175